BROADWAY THEATRE POSTERS

Wendy Nelson-Cave

SMITHMARK

This edition published in 1993
by SMITHMARK Publishers Inc.,
16 East 32nd Street
New York, New York 10016.

SMITHMARK books are available for bulk
purchase for sales promotion and premium use.
For details write or telephone the Manager of
Special Sales, SMITHMARK Publishers Inc., 16
East 32nd Street, New York, NY 10016. (212)
532-6600.

Produced by Brompton Books Corp.,
15 Sherwood Place,
Greenwich, CT 06830.

ISBN 0-8317-8752-X

Printed in Spain

10 9 8 7 6 5 4 3 2 1

Page 2: *Street Scene* (musical), 1947, poster
(Poster Collection, Theatre Arts Collection,
Harry Ransom Humanities Research
Center, The University of Texas at Austin).

BROADWAY THEATRE POSTERS

CONTENTS

INTRODUCTION

The theatre is one of the oldest and most universal of human institutions, yet the single production is transitory. The original performance is only a brief moment on the stage, but such artifacts as posters, portraits, photographs, and personal accounts can help to preserve and bring back a sense of the past production in its own day. The written text or score (where they survive) are obviously the heart of the matter: precious seeds which can be re-cultivated for succeeding generations. Although revivals must reinterpret the work in the light of current conditions, some sense of continuity with the past, particularly with works which have stood the test of time, is desirable. Happily, American theatre memorabilia is the subject of conservation and research of a high order. Such documentation as posters can provide fascinating background for theatre practitioners, as well as scholars and theatre buffs.

The American theatre, although the most recent of the great theatrical traditions of western culture to evolve, is nevertheless older than the average person would think. It is not the least of the fundamental cultural contributions which were received from Britain, and

Ion: Do you want to kill the Colonel? / I feel chock full of fight.

although the American theatre subsequently found a distinctive voice of its own, cross-fertilization with the 'mother country' continues. The first recorded theatrical performance in the New World took place in the colony of Virginia in 1665, when three amateur worthies presented a play variously referred to as *Ye Bare and ye Cubb* or *Ye Bare and ye Clubb*. Although the text does not survive, the episode is known because the three men were summoned to court on charges of licentiousness. In their own defense they re-enacted their play and were acquitted.

By 1716, Williamsburg, the colonial capital of Virginia, had a theatre, the first in the New World. In 1736 the male students of William and Mary College gave a performance of Addison's *Cato* (1713) at this theatre. It is also recorded that in the same year a – presumably professional – troupe presented a season at this theatre of Farquhar's *The Recruiting Officer* (1706) and *The Beaux' Stratagem* (1707), and Mrs Susannah Centlivre's *The Busybody* (1709). Virginia, therefore, was the birthplace of the American theatre.

The English family of actors, the Hallams, first acted in Williamsburg in 1752. Although they were not the first professional players in America, they were the first of importance, and their activities continued over 50 years. Their arrival in New York City was a very significant event in the development of the Broadway stage. Lewis Hallam the Elder arrived with his company in New York armed with a testimonial from the Governor of Virginia as to the good character of his troupe; actors had a dubious reputation right from the start, and this must have affected their publicity.

The first New York appearance of the Hallams was in Steele's *The Conscious Lovers* (1722) at the Nassau Street Theatre on September 17, 1753. The city had already seen the inferior troupe of Thomas Kean and Walter Murray in 1750 at the Nassau (the former no relation to the celebrated actor, Edmund Kean). Kean and Murray are credited with introducing professional performances to New York City; their earliest recorded

season there included Shakespeare's *Richard III*, and John Gay's *The Beggar's Opera* (1728), respectively the first tragedy and musical comedy on the New York stage. More recent scholarship has discovered reference to a performance of *The Recruiting Officer* in New York as early as 1732; although this was almost certainly by amateurs, it nevertheless stands as the first known presentation of a comedy.

The earliest extant playbills for New York are dated 1750 and describe productions of Otway's *The Orphan* (1680) and *Richard III*. Although somewhat inconclusive, they are presumed to be for the Murray/Kean company. The Nassau Street Theatre was little more than a large room, and was not purpose-built; it is thought to have been in use for only about four years. Like the original theatre in Williamsburg, very little is known of it. The means of attracting an audience then, as now, was by word-of-mouth, by displaying posters and distributing handbills, and by announcements in the press. At the time that Murray and Kean performed, George II was on the throne, Admiral George Clinton was Governor of the colony of New York, and the population of the city was about 10,000 souls.

The building of the New Theatre by the Hallams three years later specifically for performances does seem to indicate some improvement in business. Mrs Lewis Hallam was not only a woman of good character, which was important, but also the first actress of note on the New York stage. The Hallam children had acted with their parents in Williamsburg, and Lewis Hallam the Younger carried on the company with his stepfather, David Douglass after his father's death. In due course the New Theatre was re-named the John Street Theatre, and a very substantial number of their playbills survive. Early American playbills are hardly distinguishable in any important particular from their counterparts in London at the same time.

The John Street Theatre opened in December 1767, and was the first permanent playhouse in New York City. It was the venue for the staging of the first

Below left: Frontispiece to the published edition of Royall Tyler's comedy *The Contrast*, featuring the original cast.

Right: In 1753 the Hallams founded the New Theatre. This playbill for *Richard III* dates from 1753 and is one of the earliest extant playbills.

professional production by an American author, *The Prince of Parthia* (1767) by Thomas Godfrey. The Hallam/Douglass company became known as the American Company, a move which was obviously good publicity, but troubled times were ahead. In 1774 the fledgling US Congress recommended the suspension of all theatrical entertainments, and followed this up four years later with a decree prohibiting play-acting in any form. Many players, including the Hallam/Douglass troupe, sat out the Revolutionary War in Jamaica and returned after the peace.

From January 1777 to 1778, the British army took over the John Street and renamed it the Theatre Royal. The troops presented amateur theatricals there when not otherwise engaged, and this kept the spirit of the theatre alive in the city. It is also on record that General Washington's troops acted *Cato* in the field. His well-known love for the theatre was to have a considerable effect on public opinion once peace returned, because of Washington's immense prestige. In 1789, the year of his inauguration as the first President, George Washington attended three plays at the John Street Theatre; when he died in 1799, theatres were closed in mourning. Even within his lifetime, Washington appeared as an on-stage character in several American dramas. The most notable was a verse tragedy entitled *André* (1798), by William Dunlap, which dealt with the themes of treason and divided loyalties, an all-too painful issue at the time. Dunlap was to be regarded as 'the father of the American theatre,' being a prolific playwright, a painter and the first historian of the American theatre. His *André* was first given on March 30, 1798, at the elegant Park Theatre which became the principal New York showcase for 50 years.

Dunlap is said to have been inspired to take up playwriting by the first native American comedy, *The Contrast*, by Royall Tyler, which was staged at the John Street on April 16, 1787. Dunlap sketched a frontispiece for the printed text of *The Contrast*, which was seen even then as a milestone in the development of a native literary form. Prior to *The Contrast* homegrown drama had made almost no headway, and in his history Dunlap outlines the reasons. These included the immediate concern of the early settlers with the struggle for survival against nature and the indigenous peoples, followed by the necessity for political stability. The prejudice against

New-York, November 12, 1753.

By a Company of COMEDIANS,
At the New-Theatre, in *Naſſau-Street*,
This Evening, being the 12th of *November*, will be preſented,
(*By particular Deſire*)
An *Hiſtorical Play*, call'd,

King RICHARD III.

C O N T A I N I N G

The Diſtreſſes and Death of King *Henry* the VIth; the artful Acquiſition of the Crown by *Crook-back'd Richard*; the Murder of the two young Princes in the Tower; and the memorable Battle of *Boſworth-Field*, being the laſt that was fought between the Houſes of *York* and *Lancaſter*.

Richard,	by	Mr. *Rigby.*
King *Henry,*	by	Mr. *Hallam.*
Prince *Edward,*	by	Maſter *L. Hallam.*
Duke of *York,*	by	Maſter *A. Hallam.*
Earl of *Richmond,*	by	Mr. *Clarkſon.*
Duke of *Buckingham,*	by	Mr. *Malone.*
Duke of *Norfolk,*	by	Mr. *Miller.*
Lord *Stanley,*	by	Mr. *Singleton.*
Lieutenant,	by	Mr. *Bell.*
Cateſby,	by	Mr. *Adcock.*
Queen *Elizabeth,*	by	Mrs. *Hallam.*
Lady *Anne,*	by	Mrs. *Adcock.*
Ducheſs of *York,*	by	Mrs. *Rigby.*

To which will be added,
A Ballad F A R C E call'd,

The D E V I L T O P A Y.

Sir *John Loverule,*	by	Mr. *Adcock.*
Jobſon,	by	Mr. *Malone.*
Butler,	by	Mr. *Miller.*
Footman,	by	Mr. *Singleton.*
Cook,	by	Mr. *Bell.*
Coachman,	by	Mr. *Rigby.*
Conjurer,	by	Mr. *Clarkſon.*
Lady *Loverule,*	by	Mrs. *Adcock.*
Nell,	by	Mrs. *Becceley.*
Lettice,	by	Mrs. *Clarkſon.*
Lucy,	by	Miſs *Love.*

PRICES: BOX, 6*ſ.* PIT, 4*ſ.* GALLERY, 2*ſ.*

No Perſons whatever to be admitted behind the Scenes.

N. B. Gentlemen and Ladies that chuſe Tickets, may have them at Mr. Parker's and Mr. Gaine's Printing-Offices.

Money will be taken at the DOOR.

To begin at 6 o'Clock.

actors has already been referred to, but the prejudice in favor of anything from London in preference to native products was also, ironically, a factor. Some plays of native origin were actually passed off as English in the hope of ensuring a better reception, although it must be admitted that distinguishing the nationality of people in the Revolutionary period is a vexed question. The interaction between the English and American theatre continues to this day, and although it is frequently fruitful, it can also be counter-productive. *The Contrast*, although undeniably an American comedy, takes as its theme the contrasting manners of the two societies.

Most American cities of any size on the eastern seaboard had theatres in the eighteenth century, and it was not until after about 1825 that New York City became the theatrical capital. Comedies of manners and historical verse tragedies were the most common types of plays,

although musical productions were also staged. *The Contrast* and *André* are among the best examples of these styles by American authors, and although the styles are of European origin, the subject matter in these two instances is native. One type of drama which was American in both style and subject was the Indian play; this had a long life which might even be said to encompass the film Western.

The first of the Indian plays was *Tammany: or, The Indian Chief* (1794), by Mrs Anne Kemble Hatton. Not only was it the first Indian drama, it was also the first American opera, and the first play from a woman's pen to be professionally produced in America. Mrs Hatton was a sister of the celebrated actress Sarah Siddons; she emigrated to New York, married, and caused a sensation with her play. Unfortunately the text is not extant, although the playbill, some songs, and some interesting press coverage survives. Two better examples of Indian dramas

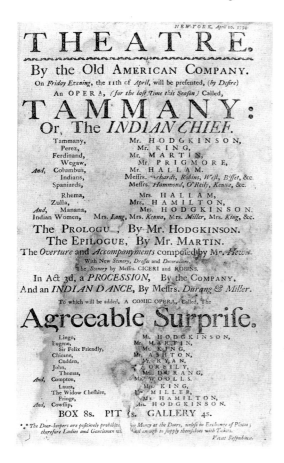

sented one of the few sources of encouragement to native playwriting at the time, as he offered a stipend for plays that he accepted.

Indian dramas have not stood the test of time but one play which has done so, and towers above all others by an American author in the nineteenth century, is *Fashion: or, Life in New York* (1845) by Mrs Anna Cora Mowatt. In her day Mrs Mowatt performed the play widely throughout America and the British Isles, and in the twentieth century *Fashion* has had several revivals in New York and elsewhere. The premiere was on March 24, 1845 at the Park Theatre. It had many imitators, but Mrs Mowatt's own later plays did not have the same impact. *Fashion* was also important in provoking some early pieces of dramatic criticism, written by the distinguished poet Edgar Allan Poe (1809-49). Anna Cora Mowatt was the great-granddaughter of a signatory to the Declaration of Independence, and she came from a socially unassailable New York family. Her decision to become an actress caused a sensation, as women of good character did not frequent theatres with regularity in her day. Her exceptionally high reputation over a period of years, both privately and professionally, had a considerable influence in improving the moral standing of the stage.

Mrs Mowatt describes in her *Autobiography of an Actress* how being taken as a young girl by her father to see the first New York appearances of Fanny Kemble (1808-93) was what inspired her to enter the theatre professionally. The high reputation of the Kembles as family people overcame her father's scruples about taking her to a theatre; no father took greater care of his actress daughter than Charles Kemble (1775-1854). American historians have credited the tours of Charles and Fanny Kemble to the theatres of the eastern seaboard in the early 1830s with putting the American theatre on a sound financial footing for the first time. Kemble made his American debut as *Hamlet*, in spite of his age, at the Park Theatre on September 17, 1832. Fanny's debut was delayed until the following night to increase audience expectation. It is perhaps not without significance that she first appeared in a play by a clergyman, the Reverend Milman's *Fazio: or, The Italian Wife*. However, father and daughter frequently acted together.

Every subsequent actress on the nineteenth-century American stage was to be

which do survive are *Metamora: or, The Last of the Wampanoages* (1829) by John Augustus Stone, and *Pocahontas: or, The Settlers of Virginia* (1830) by the first President's stepson, George Washington Parke-Curtis. Plays about Pocahontas, the Indian princess, were so common in the nineteenth century as to almost constitute a sub-genre. *Metamora* was written for the first great native-born actor, Edwin Forrest (1806-72), who acted the character for 40 years. Forrest repre-

judged by comparison with Fanny Kemble. By virtue of her long years in America and her American family connections, Fanny became looked upon as a native daughter, and her portrait now hangs in the White House. Although earlier English actors of front rank had been seen in America, the Kembles became the first full-blown stars. The star system was to gain an early ascendancy over the author of a play; it was the star, not the author, whom the public came to see, which is the principal reason why the name of the author is frequently lacking on early playbills and posters. There is a long history of English stars appearing on the New York

Below: This playbill advertising Charles and Fanny Kemble in *Hunchback* has a typically wordy typographical design.

Below: Charlotte and Susan Cushman as Romeo and Juliet, from a mid-nineteenth-century engraving; Charlotte was one of the greatest American-born stage stars of the nineteenth century.

Below: This playbill advertising Charles and Fanny Kemble in *Hunchback* has a typically wordy typographical design.

It was at about this time that theatres began to be opened on or near the street named Broadway: the New Olympic Theatre in 1812, the Anthony Street Theatre nearby in 1814, and the Bowery Theatre a few years later. The Broadway Theatre was the venue for the most distinguished American tragedy written prior to the twentieth century, *Francesca da Rimini* (1855), by George Henry Boker. The phrase 'on Broadway' had its origin in the nineteenth century for this reason, and came to symbolize the commercial theatre in the twentieth century, although few theatres have a specific Broadway address now.

The four greatest American-born stars in the nineteenth century were Edwin Forrest and Anna Cora Mowatt, Charlotte Cushman (1816-76) and Edwin Booth (1833-93). Shakespeare was almost certainly the most frequently performed author; these four stars, as well as many others, proved themselves in Shakespearean parts, but none surpassed Booth. The highpoint of his career was his record run as Hamlet, with 100 consecutive performances beginning on November 28, 1864, at the Winter Garden Theatre. This is all the more remarkable considering that the Civil War was being fought at the time. Sadly, the distin-

CHARLOTTE AND SUSAN CUSHMAN
AS
ROMEO AND JULIET.

stage, especially in Shakespeare. Prior to the Kembles the Keans also visited the United States. Edmund Kean (c.1787-1833) made his debut on Broadway as *Richard III* in 1820 and his son Charles chose the same role for his New York debut ten years later, while Mrs Charles Kean (Ellen Tree) was first seen in the city in 1836. The Keans did not make as strong an impact as the Kembles, however, and Edmund Kean alienated New York audiences by his erratic and unreliable behavior.

Below: Ada Rehan, acclaimed particularly for her performances as Shakespeare's comic heroines, in *The Taming of the Shrew*.

Bottom: John Barrymore in suitably melodramatic pose as Hamlet, a record-breaking part for him.

guished American Shakespearean tradition of the nineteenth century lost momentum later, although there were a few isolated appearances on Broadway in the twentieth century by native actors in Shakespearean roles.

Chief among these was John Barrymore's *Hamlet*, which broke the record of Booth in 1922 and was later seen in London. John Barrymore (1882-1942) was also admired in *Richard III*, but his distinguished siblings, Ethel and Lionel Barrymore, were not Shakespeareans. Ada Rehan (1860-1916) became especially noted for her performances as Shakespeare's comic heroines and was widely acclaimed as the best ever Kate in *The Taming of the Shrew*, both in America and in Stratford-upon-Avon and London. To mark this she gave her portrait in character to the Shakespeare Memorial Theatre at Stratford. Later the Lunts were to give a sparkling performance of *The Taming of the Shrew* on Broadway, although they were normally noted for modern plays. This was also true of Helen Hayes (1900-93), who excelled as Viola in *Twelfth Night* in New York. The incomparable Katherine Cornell (1898-1974) triumphed in *Romeo and Juliet* and later in *Antony and Cleopatra*, the latter offering perhaps Shakespeare's most difficult female part; no other American actress succeeded as both the young Juliet and the mature Cleopatra. Although Cornell was also noted for a series of Shavian roles such as St Joan, she was best loved as Elizabeth Barrett Browning in *The Barretts of Wimpole*

Street (1930) by Rudolph Besier, in which she toured widely. Although Shakespeare is seldom acted on Broadway by American actors now, a visit from a British company is received from time to time. In 1992 the Royal National Theatre brought its experimental production of *Richard III*, starring Sir Ian McKellan, which joined a long tradition of performances of this play in New York.

The Broadway stage has, however, pioneered two particular areas of Shakespearean production this century, the Shakespearean musical and the free open-air New York Shakespeare Festival. The best-known musicals are *The Boys from Syracuse* (1938) by Rodgers and Hart, based on *The Comedy of Errors*; *Kiss Me Kate* (1948) by Cole Porter, based on *The Taming of the Shrew*; and *West Side Story* (1957) by Leonard Bernstein and Stephen Sondheim, based on *Romeo and Juliet*. The New York Shakespeare Festival in Central Park was founded by the late Joseph Papp in 1954. Although its location and seasonal aspect mean that it perhaps does not qualify strictly speaking as Broadway theatre, it has contributed some of the most significant productions in the post-war period, some of which have transferred to Broadway. Although there are other open-air festivals, what is unique about Papp's is his idealistic policy of keeping it free, enabling him to reach audiences which would not normally come to the theatre at all, let alone to Shakespeare. It has provided a venue where stars such as George C Scott appear in plays like *Richard III* and *The Merchant of Venice* for low wages.

Shakespeare was connected with one of the most tragic episodes in the history of the New York stage, the so-called 'Astor Place Riots' in 1849. The eminent English tragedian William Charles MacReady (1793-1873) had made many appearances around America for over a quarter of a century, during which time a rivalry had built up with Edwin Forrest. The latter considered himself badly treated by supporters of MacReady when he acted in London, although it is doubtful that this was so. The two stars acted a number of the same roles, especially in Shakespeare. On the occasion of MacReady's farewell appearance at the Astor Place Opera House, riots broke out in the streets adjoining the theatre where *Macbeth* was in progress. Although Forrest was not present, either in the theatre or in the street, historians consider that the heckling and rioting by his supporters was largely at his instigation. The authorities lost control and fired into the crowds, killing at least 22 people, and MacReady had to flee the country for his life. This dramatic saga was the subject of an excellent recent play by the American playwright Richard Nelson, entitled *Two Shakespearean Actors* (1990), which ran with success, both on Broadway, and in England with the Royal Shakespeare Company.

Another tragic event concerning the theatre was the assassination of President

Abraham Lincoln at Ford's Theatre, Washington, DC, on April 14, 1865. Although this took place out of New York, it had a widespread and negative effect on the reputation of the stage. Lincoln and his wife were watching Laura Keene's company in *Our American Cousin* (1858), by Tom Taylor, when the President was shot by a misfit, John Wilkes Booth. The murderer was also an actor and the brother of Edwin Booth, who had just finished his historic run as Hamlet. The tragedy of Lincoln's death and the earlier Astor Place Riots only added to the suspicion and hostility which many members of the public felt toward the fledgling American stage. Ford's was immediately shut, and was later used as a government warehouse. A century later the Kennedy administration decided to restore it as a working theatre of its period. Ford's is thus one of the few American playhouses of nineteenth-century design to survive, and offers a good idea of what similar playhouses in New York looked like, since none of these are still standing. The design is based on the English playhouse of the eighteenth and nineteenth centuries, with a wide forestage and on-stage boxes.

It is self-evident that the mid-nineteenth century was a period of great unrest in the United States, with slavery the key issue of the day. Lincoln himself credited the novel by Harriet Beecher Stowe, *Uncle Tom's Cabin*, with exerting great influence in the fight against slavery. Mrs Stowe (1811-96) was opposed to the

theatre on moral and religious grounds and did not wish her novel to be dramatized but, due to the inadequate copyright laws of her day, she was unable to prevent this and received no income from the many enormously successful stage versions. Although her work commands great respect as a novel, it was not particularly distinguished as a stage play, but it became the most popular stage melodrama ever produced; its many stage versions were seen all over America, and even in Europe, well into the twentieth century. The initial production was the best, and was adapted by George L Aiken for the National Theatre in New York in 1853. *Uncle Tom's Cabin* marks the first time that black characters were presented as central figures in a stage play in America.

A few years later a better play took a half-breed woman as its heroine and

Below: The stage set at Ford's Theatre, Washington, DC, on the night of the assassination of President Lincoln, which exacerbated public suspicion of the fledgling stage.

Below right: Lincoln was watching *Our American Cousin* when he was shot.

Bottom: Edwin Booth as Hamlet; he had just finished his historic run of 100 consecutive performances of *Hamlet* when his crazed brother murdered Lincoln.

furthered debate on this subject which was so important in American history. *The Octoroon: or, Life in Louisiana* (1859) was by Dion Bouicicault, an excellent Irish-born playwright whose career alternated between Europe and America. *The Octoroon* is still considered a noteworthy early American drama and was revived in New York in 1961. The Civil War (1861-65) put a brake on native playwriting, although some playhouses in the north remained open during the conflict. In the second half of the century a number of plays, mostly melodramas, were inspired by the war. The best were *Shenandoah* (1889) by Bronson Howard, and William Gillette's *Held by the Enemy* (1886) and *Secret Service* (1896).

In addition to *Uncle Tom's Cabin*, two other adaptations from novels had unusually long runs and wide tours.

These were Washington Irving's *Rip van Winkle* (1864), starring Joseph Jefferson, and *Monte Cristo* (1888), based on the novel by Dumas and starring James O'Neill, father of the future playwright, Eugene O'Neill.

Another father-son combination which was important in the history of the Broadway stage was that of Steele MacKaye and his son Percy. Steele MacKaye was an 'ideas man' who became an important theatre manager, designer and playwright. He took over an old theatre and adapted it along continental lines as a repertory company, opening it as the Madison Square Theatre. Although this ambitious project eventually failed, it was here that MacKaye staged his own play, *Hazel Kirke* (1880), which had a very long Broadway run of two years before being presented internationally. A domestic drama set in England, *Hazel Kirke* was one of the most popular American plays of the period. Steele MacKaye also founded the first school of acting in New York and had a considerable influence on the theatrical scene of his day, although he had no head for business. Percy MacKaye was associated with verse drama, and his best play, *The Scarecrow* (1908), takes up the subject of witchcraft in colonial New England which was later to be tapped by Arthur Miller in *The Crucible* (1953).

Interchange with the London theatre continued after the Civil War, and mention should especially be made of the tours of the Lyceum Company with the celebrated Shakespeareans Henry Irving and Ellen Terry, who made their Broadway debut in 1881 in *The Merchant of Venice*. European stars acting in their own languages who made successful appearances in New York included Sarah Bernhardt performing in French, and Eleanora Duse in Italian.

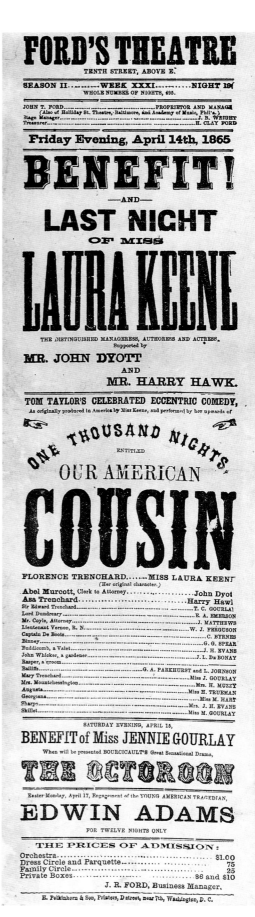

Conditions which were to lead to an increased emphasis on the writer eventually made themselves felt in New York. It is generally accepted that the Modern Drama was born with the social problem plays of the Norwegian master, Henrik Ibsen, beginning with *A Doll's House* (1879). The impact of Ibsen's work was immense across Europe and as far afield as Russia, but did not reach America for about another 40 years, with the first performances of Eugene O'Neill from 1916. Hints were heard earlier, however, with more mature subject matter, such as numerous sophisticated social comedies by Clyde Fitch, feminist plays by Rachel Crothers, and social problem plays by William Vaughn Moody and Edward Sheldon, among others. Fitch's *The Truth* (1907), Crothers' *A Man's World* (1910), Moody's *The Great Divide* (1906), and Sheldon's *Salvation Nell* (1908), *The Nigger* (1909) and *The Boss* (1911) were transitional milestones. Although tame by comparison with Ibsen and other earlier European masters, they laid the groundwork for the arrival of O'Neill. An immense amount of drama was written between the end of the Civil War and World War I; the average Broadway season in that period saw far more productions, and more Broadway theatre buildings open, than in the gradually declining situation since. A great deal of what was staged is of only marginal interest now, but with the career of Eugene O'Neill (1888-1953) the American drama matured into a recognized art form and began to catch up with trends in Europe.

The first staging of a play by O'Neill was his one-act 'sea play', *Bound East for Cardiff* (1916), which marks the birth of the American drama as a distinctive native literary form. The play was given its premiere by the then newly-formed Provincetown Players, at their summer home on Cape Cod. Later they opened a small playhouse in the Greenwich Village area of New York, and this was to become the precursor of the Off-Broadway movement. The Provincetown Players devoted themselves to discovering new American writing, and the one-act form predominated. The company was founded by the playwright Susan Glaspell, and her husband George Cram Cook. To them must go the credit for discovering and encouraging the young O'Neill and other promising writers, of whom Glaspell herself proved to be the best. The short or experimental plays of O'Neill and Glaspell were presented downtown by the Provincetown Players, but soon full-length plays by the former were being presented uptown on Broadway. O'Neill and Glaspell were the first American exponents of Expressionism, and it is significant that some of the Expressionist plays by the Swedish master August Strindberg (1849-1912) were among the few foreign works

staged at the Provincetown. Most of O'Neill's first Broadway plays, however, were in the more accessible style of Realism. O'Neill was extremely fortunate to have, in effect, his own theatre during his formative years for the staging of his experimental works. His success in the commercial arena was prompt, with his first two Broadway plays, *Beyond the Horizon* (1920), and *Anna Christie* (1921) receiving successive Pulitzer Prizes. His father, James O'Neill, lived just long enough to attend his son's Broadway debut; his only recorded response was to enquire why his son didn't write something cheerful!

WINTER GARDEN

A CONSERVATORY OF THE ARTS.

Dedicated to the culture of

COMEDY, MUSIC, BALLET,

—BY—

MISS AGNES ROBERTSON

This establishment has been newly constructed and decorated from plans and designs furnished by Mr. Dion Bourcicault.

TO-NIGHT

—AND—

EVERY NIGHT

A NEW PLAY, IN FIVE ACTS,

—BY—

Dion Bourcicault, Esq.,

The author of many popular dramatic works.

New Scenery,

Appropriate Costumes.

MR. BOURCICAULT.....as....**Wah-no-tee,** a Lepan Indian Chief
MISS AGNES ROBERTSON...as....... **Zoe,** the Octoroon
Mr. JEFFERSON.....as....**Salem Scudder,** the Yankee overseer
Mr. JOHNSTON.....as....**McCloskey,** the " piece of Connecticut hardware."
Mr. JAMIESON..(his first appearance in New York for many years).....as....**Pete,** the Old Slave
Mr. A. H. DAVENPORT.....as....**George Peyton**
Mr. G. HOLLAND...as....**Sunnyside,** the Planter
Mr. PEARSON...as....**Ratts,** mate of the Magnolia steamer
Mrs. BLAKE....as....**Madam Peyton,** the Southern Planter
Mrs. ALLEN...as....**Dora Sunnyside,** a Southern belle

TO-NIGHT

And EVERY NIGHT,

Will be performed, a new play, in five acts, illustrative of

AMERICAN CHARACTER, AMERICAN SCENES and SOUTHERN HOMES,

CALLED THE

OCTOROON

—OR—

Life in Louisiana

The scene is laid in the Delta of the Mississippi River, on the Plantation of Terrebonne, belonging to Madame Peyton, widow of the late Judge.

THE TIME—THE PRESENT WINTER.

N. B.—The Octoroon is a Southern name, given to the "eighth blood"—being the child of a quadroon by a white.

CHARACTERS:

Mrs. Peyton, of Terrebonne Plantation, in the Attakapas, widow of the late Judge Peyton.....Mrs. Blake
George Peyton, her nephew, educated in Europe, and just returned home.....Mr. A. H. Davenport
Jacob McCloskey, formerly overseer of Terrebonne, but now owner of one half of the estate.....Mr. T. B. Johnston
Salem Scudder, a Yankee from Massachusetts, now overseer of Terrebonne, great on improvements and inventions, once a photographic operator, and been a little of everything generally.....Mr. J. Jefferson
Pete, an "ole uncle," once the late Judge's body servant, but now "too ole to work, sa".....Mr. G. Jamieson
(His first appearance in New York for many years.)
Zoe, an Octoroon girl, free, the natural child of the late Judge by a Quadroon slave.....Miss Agnes Robertson
Sunnyside, a planter, neighbor and old friend of the Peytons.....Mr. G. Holland
Dora Sunnyside, his only daughter and heiress, a Southern Belle.....Mrs J. H. Allen
Lafourche, a rich Planter.....Mr. Stoddart
Wah-no-tee, an Indian Chief of the Lepan Tribe.....Mr. D. Bourcicault
Paul, a yellow boy, a favorite of the late Judge's, and so allowed to do much as he likes.....Miss Burke
Ratts, Mate of the Magnolia steamer.....Mr. H Pearson
Colonel Pointdexter, an Auctioneer and slave salesman.....Mr. Russell
Jules Thibodeaux, a young creole Planter.....Miss H. Secor
Caillou, an Overseer.....Mr. Peck
Jackson, a Planter.....Mr. Tree
Claiborne, the auctioneer's Clerk.....Mr. Ponisi
Grace, a yellow girl, a slave.....Miss Gimber
Solon, a grief boy slave.....Mr. Styles
Dido, the cook, a slave.....Mrs. Dunn
Mrs. Claiborne.....Miss Clinton
Minnie, a Quadroon slave.....Miss Walters
Planters, Slaves, Dock Hands and Ladies.

THE ARGUMENT OF THE PLAY.

Nothing extenuate, or aught set down in malice.—SHAKSPEARE.
Troe, Tyrisuro mihi nullo discrimine agetur.—VIRGIL.

SCENE OF THE FIRST ACT.

The PLANTATION of TERREBONNE.

A Southern home under a Southern sun. The little darkies, "dem's wuss dan Skeeters." Pete, the old servant. George Peyton just arrived home. A Paris lion in a canebrake. Madame Peyton and the patriarchal home. The good old Judge. Salem Scudder's description of Zoe, the Octoroon. The two overseers. A contrast. The strange relation and affection existing between Madam Peyton and her husband's natural daughter. Plantation life. Southern waste and Northern thrift. Zoe, the Octoroon. The arrival of Sunnyside and Dora. Dora Sunnyside a portrait. George cannot understand the social position of Zoe. McCloskey arrives. The hard customer. Paul, the yellow boy, and Wah-no-tee, the Indian hunter. The strange affection between the savage and the boy slave, companions in the swamp. Paul and the Indian start across the Red Cedar Swamp for the United States mail. Border United States mail delivery. The foreclosure on Terrebonne. The plantation to be sold. The last hope of recovering the estate. The Judge's desk. McCloskey's love for the Octoroon. "I cannot marry you, but I can make you mistress of the richest estate in Louisiana." The two overseers review the state of things. The live oak and the creeper. Two live Yankees, or diamond cut diamond. Scudder's confession of his love for Zoe. McCloskey discovers the free papers of Zoe. The judgment. The dark hope. The resolve.

ACT THE SECOND.

THE LANDING ON THE ATCHAFALAYA.

The Lumber Shed.

Scudder returns to his old trade and takes a photograph. Paul wants his picture took. Pete brings terrible news. Zoe confirms it. George's declaration of his love. "Say me, mas't I!" Pete on the stand. His indignation at going cheap. No. 4.—The Octoroon girl, Zoe. Consternation of the slaves. McCloskey bids. The assault by George. Bowie knives and revolvers. Dora's revenge on Zoe, who has taken away her lover. The sale of the Octoroon

ACT THE FOURTH.

THE BOILER DECK OF THE MAGNOLIA

THE LANDING AND THE WOODPILE.

Roll on the cotton bales. Take her guards under. She is freighted down into the solid mud, and can't float. No matter, 'Wood up; bang on to the safety valve; she'll crawl off on her paddles." Alarm! The Indian comes. Wah-no-tee, the murderer of Paul. Seizure of the savage. Popular fury. Lynch him! Lynch him! Scudder protects him. Paul's grave discovered, and the missing mail bags brought to light. Evidence strong.

THE LYNCH TRIAL.

Counsellor Scudder defends the Indian. Scudder on Lynch. A new witness arrives very unexpectedly. An alteration of the entertainments for that evening. Scudder on McCloskey. Improved and corrected Edition. McCloskey is a fix. The verdict and the seizure of the prisoner. McCloskey's escape.

THE SHED ON FIRE.

Cut the ropes. Back her out. Clear away. The criminal away. His Indian destiny pursues him.

The Destruction of the Steamer Magnolia by Fire

The vessel swings in the stream a prey to the flames.

ACT THE FIFTH.

Scene First.—The Negro Quarter—Night.
Zoe seeks her old nurse, Dido. The old Obi Doctress. The drink that cures the Red Fever. The night after the sale. Life is so beautiful to one so young.

Scene Second.—The Cane Brake—Sunrise.
McCloskey out of danger. His flight through the swamps. His escape. The dusky shadow of death behind him. The Indian on the war path. The pursuit. The human bloodhound.

Scene Third.—The Red Cedar Swamp.
Scudder and Pete on their road home. What's that in the bush. "A Rat or a runaway Nigger." The man hunt. The wolf run down at last. The Indian and his victim. Save me from the scalping knife of the savage. Judge Scudder's revision of the lynch verdict. His decision. Pete's petition. Scudder relents. His protection of the white man.

Scene Fourth, and Last.
The parlor at Terrebonne again. Zoe's adieu to her home while she leaves it for the house of her new master. The glass of water. The arrival of scudder. The joyful news. Pete in a bad way. Zoe's freedom. Free at last.

THE OCTOROON GOES HOME

THE VISION OF THE LANDING.

LITTLE PAUL'S GRAVE.

McCloskey appeals to the highest tribunal. The last that was seen of the Indian Wah-no-tee.

During the winter season, the doors will open at Six P. M. The entertainments commence at Seven.

Families bringing children are informed that the entertainments always conclude before half-past Ten o'clock. This rule will only be departed from under particular circumstances, and this departure will be notified in the bills.

PRICES OF ADMISSION :

Dress Circle and Parquette	50 Cents
Family Circle	25 Cents
Orchestra Stalls	One Dollar
Private Boxes	Seven Dollars

Box office is open at 8 A. M., and Seats may be secured and tickets purchased until Six P. M.
When the Theatre is full, notice will be placed at the entry. No seats will be allowed to occupy the ailey ways and passages, such a practice being deemed inconsistent with the comfort and convenience of the audience.
Seats may be secured six days in advance.
Attached to the Parquette lobby is a handsome Saloon where wines, &c., of excellent quality may be obtained.

HERALD PRINT.

Below: Playwright Eugene O'Neill, photographed in 1938. The advent of writers such as O'Neill heralded a renewed emphasis on the role of the author on Broadway.

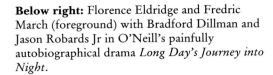

Below right: Florence Eldridge and Fredric March (foreground) with Bradford Dillman and Jason Robards Jr in O'Neill's painfully autobiographical drama *Long Day's Journey into Night.*

Below: Playwright Eugene O'Neill, photographed in 1938. The advent of writers such as O'Neill heralded a renewed emphasis on the role of the author on Broadway.

Gradually the reputation of Eugene O'Neill became secure enough for his Broadway management, the Theatre Guild, to risk staging his nine-act Expressionist drama, *Strange Interlude* (1928), on Broadway. With Lynn Fontanne (b.1887) in the central role audiences were, perhaps, a little more prepared to endure the play's length, which required an early start and a dinner interval. Not only the extreme length, but O'Neill's experimental approach to the dialogue, whereby all the characters spoke not only their conversation but their inner thoughts, stretched the boundaries of what the typical Broadway audience was used to accepting. Although *Strange Interlude* won O'Neill his third Pulitzer Prize and marked the end of his busiest decade as a dramatist, the best was yet to come. Greek tragedy had served as the inspiration for his controversial and shocking farm tragedy, *Desire Under the Elms* (1924), but he undertook a far more ambitious use of myth in his trilogy *Mourning Becomes Electra* (1931). Reinterpreting *The Oresteia* of Aeschylus for a New England setting at the time of the Civil War, O'Neill cast his saga in 11 acts. This period of his life culminated in the receipt of the Nobel Prize for Literature in 1934.

The significance of O'Neill's work lies both in his efforts to raise the American drama to the level of high tragedy, and his experimentation with literary and stage techniques. He stretched the boundaries of the form, and while few would deny him the honor of being 'the father of American Drama,' it is not so frequently remarked that he also raised the standard of American dramatic criticism. His work

sent the critics back to school and, if some found his forays into Greek tragedy, his use of masks, choruses, interior monologues and so on, pretentious, O'Neill nevertheless had to be judged on his own terms. He took the very highest model the history of the theatre has produced as his principal inspiration. He had seemingly retired from the theatre in the 1930s and some people even thought he was dead. World War II deeply depressed him and this, together with ill health, resulted in his becoming virtually a recluse. Just after the war his surprise return was heralded by a rare press conference which introduced *The Iceman Cometh* (1946). This was the last of his works to be staged on Broadway within O'Neill's lifetime and, like much of what he had already written,

was heavily autobiographical. Running for about four hours, *Iceman* was an uncompromisingly bleak tragedy of low life set in a New York bar in 1912. It depicted the same setting and era used in *Anna Christie*, but the new play was of an infinitely more philosophical nature and is now recognized as one of the seminal works of Modern Drama.

A more closely autobiographical tragedy was *Long Day's Journey into Night*, which may have been written as early as 1941, but was not staged until 1956. The author dedicated the text to his wife with the note that it had been 'written in blood and tears,' and instructed that it should be withheld until 25 years after his death. Dealing with O'Neill's drug-addicted mother, his alcoholic actor-

father and brother, and his tubercular self, the play is painfully personal. O'Neill's widow permitted the staging only a few years after her husband's death, but assigned the premiere to a Swedish theatre. *Long Day's Journey into Night* opened in New York at the Helen Hayes Theatre on November 7, 1956. It had a prestigious cast, including the husband-and-wife team of Fredric March and Florence Eldridge, with Jason Robards Jr as the young O'Neill.

The play is the quintessential American drama, drawing together the story of the father, an important representative of the nineteenth-century theatre, with that of the son who was the founder of the twentieth-century tradition. The play also takes in the larger theme of the immigrant family in the New World, a theme which has been basic to American literature. Universally recognized now as the greatest of all American plays, *Long Day's Journey into Night* won a posthumous New York Drama Critics' Circle Award and O'Neill's fourth Pulitzer Prize, and set in motion what became known as 'the O'Neill revival.' Robards has been central to this for many years and has become the leading interpreter of O'Neill's late or posthumous plays, of which there were several. Although *Long Day's Journey* dispenses with legends, masks, choruses and the like, it comes closer than any other modern play to re-casting the philosophical essence of Greek tragedy for the contemporary stage. During his 40 years as a playwright between 1916 and 1956, O'Neill brought a new seriousness to the Broadway stage and forged a place for American drama in serious repertories around the world.

Space precludes more than a brief mention of other noteworthy writers of the twentieth-century Broadway stage. Non-American dramatists other than Shakespeare must be omitted, except for George Bernard Shaw, who developed a singular connection with Broadway, and whose immense prestige requires a brief note of that connection. Shaw's satire on the American Revolution, *The Devil's Disciple* (1897), was given its premiere on Broadway by the American actor Richard Mansfield. The comedy was so successful that the income enabled Shaw to give up journalism in London and devote his entire attention to playwriting. Shaw subsequently contracted with the Theatre Guild to present in New York the premieres of what are now regarded as his two best works, *Heartbreak House* (1920) and *St Joan* (1923). The Guild also staged

the premiere of what Shaw alone considered his masterpiece, *Back to Methusaleh* (1922).

To return to American dramatists, one of the most admired in the 1930s and later was Maxwell Anderson. Early in his career he collaborated with Laurence Stallings on what was seen as the best American anti-war play, *What Price Glory?* (1924), which introduced the frank dialogue of soldiers in the trenches to shocked audiences. Undertaking a drastic change of style, Anderson later became the principal exponent in America of the verse revival, and wrote a whole series of historical plays in poetry. But his real innovation came when he applied blank-verse dialogue to contemporary characters in *Winterset* (1935) and *High Tor* (1937). The former, failing to achieve a Pulitzer Prize, was considered so

important that the New York Drama Critics' Circle Award was created and *Winterset* was the first recipient. The award was also given to *High Tor*. Taking up the challenge of Expressionism, Elmer Rice wrote one of the most original dramas of the Broadway stage with *The Adding Machine* (1924). Although his *Street Scene* (1929) reverted to the more conventional style of Realism, it was still a memorable drama of the stresses of modern life. Lillian Hellman was also a challenging new playwright and her first work, *The Children's Hour* (1930), was exceptionally daring, even dealing in a subtle manner with lesbianism. Her best play, *The Little Foxes* (1939), set her work firmly in the Southern milieu which was later also to supply the background for the plays of Tennessee Williams.

Writing in the style known in Europe as Pirandellian but in America as Theatricalism, Thornton Wilder contributed two outstandingly original plays to Broadway with *Our Town* (1938) and *The Skin of Our Teeth* (1942). It was a pity that Wilder, like William Saroyan, divided his talent between drama and fiction and thus deprived the stage of further works of such a high standard. Saroyan's *The Time of Your Life* (1939) stands high in the annals of the New York stage. Some dramatists of note were less than prolific, but Robert E Sherwood wrote a whole series of respected plays, including *Idiot's Delight* (1936), performed by the Lunts, and *Abe Lincoln in Illinois* (1938), starring Raymond Massey.

Some American comedy was written in collaboration, and especially enjoyable were the zany works of George S Kaufman with his various partners. The best was *You Can't Take It With You* (1936), which he wrote with Moss Hart. A wag once described American comedy as the comedy of bad manners, and no play better exemplifies that than Clare Boothe Luce's *The Women* (1936). This comedy had a very large all-female cast which, together with some unusual choices of setting such as a ladies' hairdressing salon and a private bathroom, gave it considerable novelty at the time. High comedy of good manners was not lacking, for example Philip Barry's *The Philadelphia Story* (1939). Fantasy as a genre is a very rare form of comedy, and one of the all-time great examples in Broadway history was Mary Chase's *Harvey* (1944). So unique was her treatment of the time-honored theme of illusion versus reality that Harvey, her eight-foot-tall invisible white rabbit, actually defeated Williams' *The Glass Menagerie* for the Pulitzer Prize.

Coming to the fore just before the death of O'Neill were the two playwrights best equipped to take up his mantle, Tennessee Williams and Arthur Miller. They represent the Southern and Northern Realist traditions respectively. Williams may be said to have been influenced by the Russian dramatist Anton Chekhov (1860-1904), while Miller is strongly in the Ibsenite vein, but both Williams and Miller acknowledged their debt to O'Neill. This influence can best be seen in their use of Expressionistic devices to heighten Realism, and in their attempts to tap the vein of tragedy. Although there is no doubt that *Death of a Salesman* (1949) is Miller's masterwork, opinion would differ as to whether *The Glass Menagerie* (1944) or *A Streetcar Named Desire* (1947) represents the best of Williams. Although Miller is America's greatest living playwright, it can perhaps now be assumed that he will not be as prolific as Williams. The best of Miller's other work is *All My Sons* (1947), *The Crucible* (1953), *A View from the Bridge* (1955), and *The Price* (1966). Miller has been awarded two New York Drama Critics' Circle Awards and one Pulitzer Prize. Williams' third-best play is probably *Cat on a Hot Tin Roof* (1955), for which he won his second Pulitzer Prize.

It was well into the twentieth century before the very high production standards for which Broadway is justly famed were fully developed. The rise of the director from about 1880 in Europe and the advent of electricity revolutionized the technical side of theatre. Directional control and the artistic use of lighting together achieved a unity of style within the production which enabled the best modern writers to see a realization of their works which had not been possible in former times, no matter how brilliant the acting. Miller and Williams had the services of an exceptionally talented set designer, Jo Mielziner (1901-76). His scenery was first seen to effect in *The Guardsman* (1924), starring the Lunts, and later included many notable productions, from Shakespeare to musicals. Mielziner's designs for *Winterset*, *A Streetcar Named Desire* and especially *Death of a Salesman* represent milestones of the scenic art; the last is frequently cited as the single most outstanding scenic design in Broadway history. With the Finnish architect Eero Saarinen, Jo Mielziner also designed the Vivian Beaumont Theatre in the Lincoln Center for the Performing Arts. With its thrust stage design, this is the only new, indoor theatre to open in New York in a Broadway context this century, and its first production was Miller's *After the Fall* (1964), for which Mielziner designed the set.

Below: Marlon Brando and Jessica Tandy in Williams' *A Streetcar Named Desire* (1947).

Bottom: Kim Hunter (left in white), Jessica Tandy (center) and Marlon Brando (right) against Mielziner's brooding, powerful set for *Streetcar*.

Streetcar, *Salesman*, and *Cat on a Hot Tin Roof* also had the benefit of one of Broadway's best modern directors, Elia Kazan (b.1909), but in spite of being able to command the top talent to enhance their plays, both Miller and Williams grew disenchanted with conditions on Broadway. Critics and public seemed to see their later plays as less good than their earlier ones, while the authors regarded their audiences as unwilling to accept new directions from their hands. Edward Albee (b.1928) was to find himself in agreement with them when, after the success of his earlier prize plays, *Who's Afraid of Virginia Woolf* (1962) and *A Delicate Balance* (1966), the reception of his later plays eroded his position as the potential successor to Miller and Williams. Times were changing and the public seemed to want relatively unchallenging light comedies, such as flowed endlessly from the pen of Neil Simon (b.1927), or musicals. The decline and death of 'the great white way', as Broadway is sometimes called, has been repeatedly predicted. The reasons for this are various, and include the advent of films and television, inner-city crime, lack of tax subsidy for the theatre, and abuse of union power. The conservatism of Broadway audiences, which renders them less open to new or experimental writing, is perhaps to some extent understandable, considering the increasingly high cost of tickets. Coincident with a decline in the number of good straight plays being produced was a marked and steady improve-

ment in the standard of the musical, and this was to become the more dominant form of theatre in New York.

The American musical comedy has sometimes been derisively called the country's only original contribution to the long history of world theatre. Its origin is to be found in the English classic, *The Beggar's Opera* (1728) which was, as mentioned earlier, the first musical to be presented on the New York stage. Gay's work was known as a ballad-opera, a form containing both new music written specially for it and also ballads taken from other sources. A ballad-opera must have spoken dialogue, rather than recitative, and it must have a comic plot. The original London production at the Theatre Royal, Covent Garden was one of the first long runs in history and was very soon revived. Staged in New York in 1750, it was to have a number of American imitators.

Below: Producer and showman Florenz Ziegfeld was notable both for his lavish musical productions, which included *Showboat* (1927), and for the *Ziegfeld Follies*, spectacular and exotic revues which he staged for 24 years.

ductions too the lavish and revealing costumes of the showgirls were the chief attraction to the public.

The mention of George M Cohan would start many Americans' toes tapping. Apart from Edwin Booth, Cohan is the only theatrical figure to be commemorated by a statue in New York City. Cohan's career roughly coincided with those of several well-known composers of American operettas, such as Victor Herbert, Rudolph Friml, and Sigmund Romberg, who wrote many lovely songs but whose productions tended to look back to a rather old-fashioned European model. The musicals of George M Cohan, however, were set in America, and were highly idiomatic and patriotic. His tempo was energetic, up-beat, and singularly 'New York' in style. Cohan's song, 'Give My Regards To Broadway,' is the quintessential American show tune. Among his more successful musicals were *45 Minutes to Broadway* (1906), and *The Song and Dance Man* (1913). He himself made a few noteworthy appearances as an actor in straight plays. In 1968 the musical *George M*, based upon his career, was produced on Broadway.

Cohan was a one-off original; in the post-World War I era, an increasing number of musicals were being written by collaboration. At first many of these collaborations were by two figures representing the past and present styles respectively, such as Victor Herbert/Irving Berlin; Victor Herbert/Jerome Kern; Sigmund Romberg/Richard Rodgers; Sigmund Romberg/George Gershwin. This seems to emphasize that the musical form was in a transitional phase from the old-style operetta to the newer, more energetic type of show focusing on American subject matter. In due course, the former lost ground.

A major turning point was *Show Boat* (1927), which was based on a novel by Edna Ferber. Her book took up serious themes such as miscegenation, prejudice, adultery and murder, and these were by no means glossed over in the musical written by Jerome Kern and Oscar Hammerstein II. Indeed, 'Ole Man River' and other songs not only brilliantly integrated these themes into believable characterizations, but were technically evocative of the music of the Civil War period in which the production was set. Such artistic musicals as *Show Boat*, and later *Of Thee I Sing* (1931), were moving the American musical more and more toward a finely balanced integration of song,

The Black Crook (1866) was by no means an imitator, being a totally different type of presentation, but it has rightly become legendary as the first important American musical. *The Black Crook*, by Charles M Barras, was the first native work successfully to combine music, dance and plot. This melodramatic fairy-tale was dismissed by *The New York Tribune* in 1866 as 'rubbish,' but one need only look at the posters and other illustrations to see that it was impressive as pure spectacle. The original *Black*

Crook set a record for its time, running at the Niblo's Garden Theatre for 445 performances. It was revived at the same place in 1881, and at other times and places as well. It was part ballet, and acquired a somewhat naughty reputation on account of the many beautiful, but very skimpy, costumes worn by the female dancers. In this regard it may be seen as the precursor of the *Ziegfeld Follies* and the *George White Scandals*, which were to enliven the Broadway scene in repeated editions in the early twentieth century. In these pro-

dance, plot and character which was lacking in earlier productions. *Of Thee I Sing*, which deals with the theme of American elections, was the first musical deemed worthy to receive the Pulitzer Prize, normally reserved for straight drama. The creators were a formidable team: music by George Gershwin, with lyrics by his brother Ira, and the book by George S Kaufman and Morrie Ryskind.

Completely separate from these trends, or indeed any trends, was a musical drama entitled *Four Saints in Three Acts* (1934), with a Dadaist-Surrealist text by Gertrude Stein and a score by Virgil Thompson. With an all-black cast and decor by a highly original artist, Florine Stettheimer (1871-1944), this completely obscure abstraction, which attempted to blur the distinction between literature, painting and music, caused a sensation but inspired no imitators.

The following year, a totally different all-black musical drama was produced in New York which was also outside the mainstream of developments. Perhaps Gershwin's *Porgy and Bess* (1935) is more accurately termed a folk opera, but there is no doubt it is one of the most distinguished works in Broadway history. Based upon a good straight play by DuBose and Dorothy Heyward entitled *Porgy*, the work features music by Gershwin which stands on an even higher plane than the sparkling best of his 'Tin Pan Alley' type of musical, such as *Lady Be Good* (1924) and *Oh, Kay!* (1926).

The 1930s saw further experimentation in the musical, but it is generally agreed that the most important milestone in the

genre was *Oklahoma!* (1943). Both Richard Rodgers and Oscar Hammerstein had written memorable work with previous partners, but now as a team they were to set the standard for years to come. *Oklahoma!* opened on March 31, 1943, at the St James Theatre and it lifted the mood of a war-weary nation, since the songs were widely heard across the country by millions who could not attend the show.

In addition to achieving to perfection the integration of the various elements

towards which the form had been moving, *Oklahoma!* also incorporated the brilliant choreography of Agnes de Mille, taking the dance element to an artistic level not seen before. From now on, dance had to be structurally built in to the story to advance the plot, as well as to delineate characterizations. Songs and dances could no longer merely pop out at intervals just to liven things up; these elements had to emerge for a reason and be well-motivated. 'A seamless web' was the analogy used to describe *Oklahoma!*, and henceforth not only Rodgers and Hammerstein but others too were to emphasize the book-musical. Interestingly enough, in more recent times dance has begun to recede again in certain musicals. Critics noted its almost total absence from Alan Jay Lerner and Frederick Loewe's *My Fair Lady* (1956), a musical milestone by any reckoning. Of course this did have an unusually strong literary text, and perhaps the omission of dance was a concession to the shade of Bernard Shaw, who would have objected to any musical adaptation of *Pygmalion* (1913).

Some of Stephen Sondheim's work, such as *Sunday in the Park With George* (1984), has also taken this route. Both this work and *My Fair Lady* deal largely with intellectual ideas which are not easily expressed by dance. Sondheim's musicals, which are ultra-modern and highly inventive, now seem to some observers to

Below: Letterpress playbill for the distinguished tragedy *Francesca da Rimini* (1855), which doubled as a program and therefore included the maximum amount of information.

be the way forward for the musical in an American context. His first Broadway breakthrough was as lyricist for Leonard Bernstein's brilliantly re-told *Romeo and Juliet*, *West Side Story* (1957). His talent developed further with a series of productions including *Follies* (1971), *Sweeney Todd* (1979), *Into The Woods* (1986) and others, but *Sunday in the Park With George* is looked upon as the first truly modernist Broadway musical, and it won the Pulitzer Prize. The subject is adapted from the life of the French artist Georges Seurat (1859-91), and the production displayed one of those technical feats for which Broadway is noted, the gradual bringing to life of an exact rendering of Seurat's famous painting, *Sunday Afternoon on the Island of La Grande Jatte*, now in the Chicago Art Institute. Gertrude Stein would have loved it!

In the present tough, commercial arena of Broadway, not only straight plays but

musicals are finding it hard going to make a profit. Significantly the British, with whom it all began, are back in force, exploiting the long-standing American inferiority complex in the face of culture from 'the mother country.' The rise of the British musical has challenged Broadway on its home ground, and many straight plays from London are now also seen in New York. Unseemly squabbles between British and American Equity have not produced a positive, longterm policy concerning exchanges. It may yet prove more fruitful to return to the situation before the two traditions of the Anglo-American theatre split, and simply let any production which can get and hold an audience do so in either London or New York. The play with the most enduring popularity on Broadway may yet prove to be *Richard III* (1750-1992)!

Every live performance obviously requires an audience, for the theatre is a form of communication. Some publicity, therefore, has always been a prerequisite, even as far back as the classical theatres of Greece and Rome. Playbills, programs, and posters are all types of publicity communicating information on performances. The early printed playbills were small and used the method known as letterpress, whereby letters were cut in reverse and were then inked and printed by means of a handpress. This system had originated in the fifteenth century, but letterpress remained in use in the theatre until the nineteenth century. As in many other areas of theatre practice, the fledgling American stage followed the precedent of England. By the seventeenth century larger playbills were in use in England, and these were the antecedent of the modern theatre poster. In the mid-eighteenth century the playbill to be displayed in various public places, and also dispensed inside the playhouse like a modern program, was also in use in America. This dual-purpose item was at first entirely in words, and printed by letterpress. The program/playbill used variously sized letters, the larger letters for the more important information, especially the title of the play and the name of the star. The name of the author, as explained earlier, was frequently omitted. These early black-and-white broadsides would also very often use larger letters to add superlatives or glowing adjectives, which would inform the reader that the performance was 'sensational,' the star 'eminent,' the scenery

'spectacular,' and so on. The arrangement for the various mixed typographical forms could effect an attractive visual pattern on these early broadsides even before illustrations as such were in use. The average size of an early playbill was about 7 x 22 inches (18 x 46 cm).

These early examples were crudely printed, and the heavy, black ink would easily bleed through or smear. They were often printed on cheap paper, and it is amazing that so many fragile examples have survived in specialist library collections. Although much of the paper advertising from the advent of the American stage until the present was expected to be quickly disposable, private and public collections grew up containing vast numbers of these flimsy playbills, and later the somewhat sturdier cardboard posters. These collections became invaluable to scholars, theatre practitioners and other interested parties, and now form a very important part of the historical record of general developments, as well as a record of the particular performance which, in itself, was so highly perishable. The letterpress playbill had become more sophisticated by the mid-nineteenth century, when woodcut and wood-engraved images were added to the words, and colored inks and papers were beginning to be used more frequently. The rough woodcut might incorporate a simple likeness of the star, or a decorative motif suggestive of the theme of the play. The earlier black-and-white typographical playbill had the disadvantage (especially when used as a display poster) of being rather difficult and time-consuming to read. Not only were they a bit hard on the eyes, but one needs to bear in mind that possibly even as late as the nineteenth century some potential patrons may have been unable to read. The introduction of color and illustrations, with a corresponding reduction in words, eased these problems and made a more immediate impact on passing trade.

The earliest extant New York City playbills date from the 1750s. The arrival of the first English actors in the city needed advertising vigorously; they were breaking new ground and had to contend with the Puritan ethic of the native audience, which rendered them hostile to actors and play-acting on religious and moral grounds. By the end of the nineteenth century, materialism, education, and a wider religious base in the population of New York City resulted in improved conditions for the theatre.

Below: Letterpress playbill for *Hamlet*, starring Edwin Booth.

Below right: Playbill for Cordelia Howard as Little Eva in *Uncle Tom's Cabin* (1858).

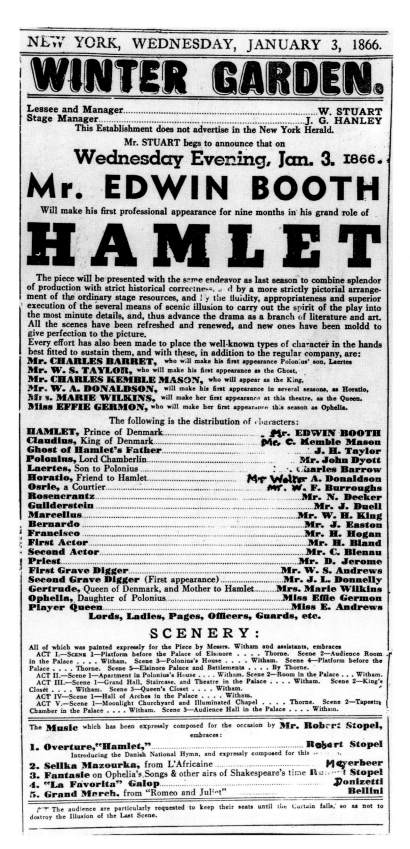

Gradually native pride produced a desire for homegrown arts – literary, musical, visual – which in turn contributed to an improvement in the standards of theatre advertising.

By about 1820, the method of printing known as lithography had reached America. This was not a relief method of printing, like the earlier methods of letterpress or woodcut; lithography printed from a damp, flat limestone upon which the image had been inscribed with a greasy, crayon-type writing tool. Each color required a separate printing. A lithograph is in effect a crayon drawing on stone, but by means of the printing press may be multiplied as often as needed. The crayon contains tallow which sinks into the stone where touched by the crayon. When the drawing is completed, the surface of the stone is covered by weak nitric acid. The acid does not make any incision in the stone; it is used to clean up ungreased areas. The stone must be kept moist during the process. Since water and grease do not mix, the parts drawn upon will repel water, and the parts not drawn upon will absorb it. A roller charged with greasy ink is then passed over the surface. A sheet of paper is placed upon the stone, which is then passed through the press. The ink, affixing to the paper, produces a facsimile of the artist's drawing in reverse.

The introduction of printed programs to be distributed within the theatre allowed the playbill/poster to omit some

Below: In the second half of the nineteenth century the poster began to emphasize visual elements of the production. The work of Alphonse Mucha (1860-1939) helped to establish the artistic poster; this is Mucha's design for a poster advertising Maude Adams in *Joan of Arc* (see page 50).

Nathanial Currier began publishing highly colored prints in America in 1840, and his success established him as the front-runner in the field. In 1852 James Ives joined his firm. The famous Currier and Ives prints were lithographs, hand-colored on a mass-production basis; for about half a century this firm published three new prints per week, on every aspect of American life. The American artist Joseph W Morse was also noteworthy, in the 1840s and later, for creating multi-colored posters. He specialized in the circus, using cuts in pine which were cheaper than the cuts used previously for circus posters, and he printed the poster in small sections with a different block of wood for each color of his design. In those days, travelling circuses were far more common. One of Morse's posters, for the Hawes and Cushing Circus which was performing in England, is said to have come to the attention of the French artist Jules Chéret (1836-1932), who was engaged in England at the time. Upon Chéret's return to Paris in 1866 he began creating work along the lines of Morse, and this was one of the influences which led to Chéret being known as 'the father of the modern poster.'

M B Leavitt, a theatrical manager in America, claimed in his autobiography to have introduced continental-style lithographed posters to America in 1872. Leavitt states that he bought a supply of one-color pictorial lithographs in Europe and used them for his shows in America. This created interest and, according to Leavitt, demand for a more artistic American show poster. By about 1880, lithographed posters had all but supplanted the earlier types. Companies like Strobridge Lithographing Company of Cincinnati, Ohio, and New York became pioneers and leaders for about 50 years. Not only circuses, but also touring companies of legitimate drama were much more common across America prior to World War I than since. For various reasons outside the scope of this discussion, the so-called 'road' dried up after this time. In the heyday of touring, posters for popular shows like *Uncle Tom's Cabin* were run off in bulk to the same design by firms such as Strobridge, then placed in temporary storage until the appropriate time for shipping to individual clients. The client would then fill in the local data on the pre-printed but incomplete poster. Early theatrical posters usually depicted highly dramatic scenes from the play, to whet the appetite of the potential audience.

information, which would now appear in the program instead. In other words, the old-time black-and-white broadside doubling as both poster and program separated into two pieces of paper serving two functions. The item for exterior use had the purpose of getting patrons into the theatre, whereas the interior item was intended to provide additional information to aid their understanding and enjoyment once they were there. This separation

enabled the poster for exterior use to emphasize visual elements increasingly, as technology advanced to produce the means to do so. As the emphasis on the pictorial elements of posters increased, more serious artists became involved. This resulted in higher artistic standards, although a poster should never be thought of as a painting, but only in the context of the specific publicity campaign to which it belongs.

In addition to bringing European posters to America, Leavitt also took Strobridge posters to Europe, where they created quite an impression. He states that Strobridge lithographs were the first 'high class' show printing used in Europe. Leavitt's memoir, *Fifty Years in Theatrical Management: 1859-1909*, was published in 1912, and is an invaluable account of a formative period in the American theatre, although the book makes no pretense to be scholarly. The principal designer at Strobridge for many years was Matt Morgan, who was born in England in 1836 and apprenticed as a scenery painter. After joining Strobridge, Morgan became one of the few early poster designers who was allowed to sign his work. He was an innovator, and toned down the brashness of the nineteenth-century American show poster as he found it. He trained a team, and had made a considerable impact on the development of the theatre poster by the time he left the firm. Other developments followed. By the turn of the century, lithography in America was adapted to the offset process, using photographic techniques. Another milestone was the introduction of silkscreen printing in England in the early twentieth century, with further developments in America.

As the 'road' continued to shrink, more and more theatrical activity was centered in New York City. Poster production retrenched to New York addresses, such as the Artcraft Lithograph and Printing Company, founded in Manhattan in 1922,

which was the principal successor to Strobridge. The average size of a lithographed poster settled at 14 x 22 inches (36 x 56.3 cm), twice the length of the average early playbill.

The most typical modern style of fine and applied art which emerged at the turn of the century was Art Nouveau; the posters of the Czech artist Alphonse Mucha (1860-1939) represent one of the most characteristic and best-loved manifestations of this style. The most celebrated of Mucha's work was for the great French actress, Sarah Bernhardt (1845-1923), who commissioned Mucha's first successful poster, *Gismonda* (1894), which made the artist's name in Paris. The 'divine Sarah' first acted on Broadway in 1880, and made a number of subsequent tours of America. When Mucha accompanied her to New York in 1894, his work made its greatest impact in America. His beautifully romantic posters of Bernhardt give a fragile, delicate impression. Mucha is on record, however, as considering American women more beautiful because they were more robust, and it is therefore interesting to see what he made of two American actresses, Leslie Carter and Maude Adams, for whom he designed posters in 1908 and 1909.

Mucha designed costumes, scenery and the poster for *Kassa*, by John Luther Long, which starred Mrs Carter (1862-1937) and opened on Broadway on January 22, 1909 after an out-of-town tour. The poster was also used for the program cover, and no writing appears except the star's name. Shortly after, Mucha designed a poster for Maude Adams (1872-1963) in *Joan of Arc*, choosing to show the saint in a girl's peasant dress rather than armor. In this case her name and the (erroneous) title of Schiller's play, *The Maid of Orleans*, appears but no other writing, not even the name of such a distinguished playwright.

Until 1894 the artistic poster was hardly known in the United States, but from that time the posters of Mucha, and also of the English artist Aubrey Beardsley (1872-98), were among the influences which were to make a strong impression in America. It has even been suggested that the Art Nouveau designs of Beardsley became more 'the rage' in America than in his native England. Beardsley had several American imitators; Will Bradley (1868-1962), for example, became known in some circles as 'the American B' in reference to his similarity to Beardsley's style, and even seems to have challenged

Beardsley on his home ground by designing one of his best posters for an English play, *The Masqueraders* (1894) by Henry Arthur Jones, which was seen in London but not in New York. Other outstanding American designers at the turn of the century and slightly later include Edward Penfield, Ethel Reed, Frank Hazenplug and William L Carqueville. Later still, Charles Dana Gibson, Howard Chandler Christy, E McKnight Kauffer and Norman Rockwell were very much in demand for various forms of commercial art, including posters. While none of the artists mentioned worked exclusively in posters, their influence was wide. But it should be reiterated that the theatrical poster takes its line of descent from the black-and-white playbill featuring a cast list, which was first in use in America in the mid-eighteenth century. It gradually incorporated the visual influences of posters designed for other areas of life, but due to the connection with the playbill/program discussed earlier, the American theatre poster for literary works has a slightly different evolution from other posters.

In addition to Art Nouveau and the more common style of Realism, other art styles came to public attention between about 1908 and 1917. These include Cubism, Expressionism (related to Expressionism as a dramatic style), Constructivism, and Surrealism. The various modern art movements in painting did cross-fertilize with poster design, but in

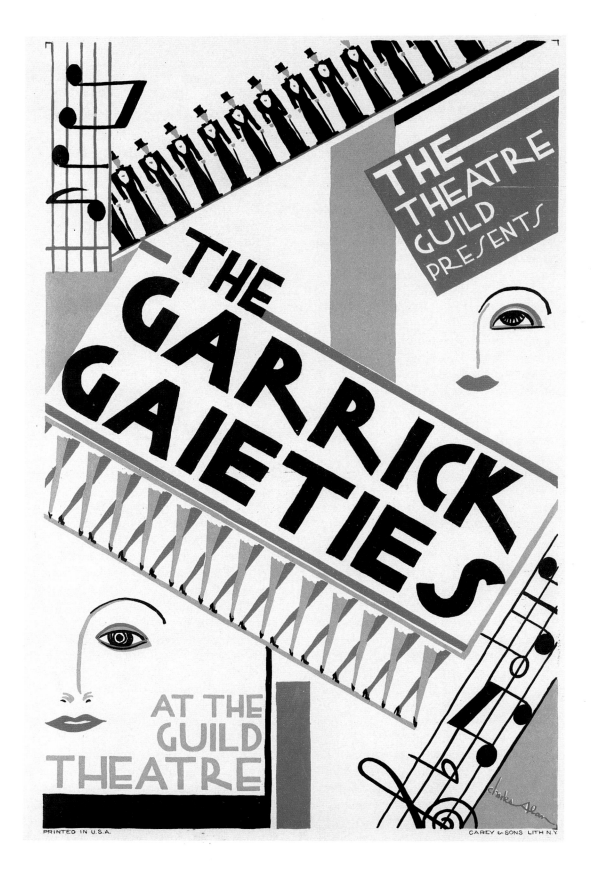

America Realism was traditionally the dominant style, both in drama and art, because it was more accessible to the patron and thus better suited to selling a product, be it a performance or another product. After World War II, however, the development of Abstract Expressionism, which was largely New York-based, enabled American art to take the lead for the first time. As consumers were becoming more sophisticated, this new American style in painting was poised to

produce a more telling affinity with largescale posters and billboards. Abstract Expressionist painting *was* typically large and bold. The New York painters were searching for a combination of abstract form with psychological content. American artists noted for this style include Willem and Elaine de Kooning, Jackson Pollock, Lee Krasner, Mark Rothko and Helen Frankenthaler.

The Theatre Guild, founded in New York City in 1919, was the chief commer-

cial producer of non-musicals on the Broadway stage for many years. The Guild set a high standard for its posters, especially in the 1920s and 1930s. One of its guiding lights and most regular and successful poster designers was the scenic artist Lee Simonson (1888-1967), an author on his craft and one of the best set designers in Broadway history. In more recent years, it has become common for the set designer also to design the poster for that production. Tony Walton, Doug Johnson, Gilbert Lesser, Hilary Knight and David Stone Martin are a few of the talented practitioners in the field of theatre posters for Broadway in recent times.

Today the poster designer is given the script to read at an early stage, and may be requested to attend the first read-through of the text, at which the actors read their parts, the director conducts a discussion on his interpretation, and the designers of costumes, scenery and lighting present their ideas. This first rehearsal is a 'sit-down' affair which might also include the author and composer, if living. The purpose of this traditional first reading is to enable the director to start off his team in unity, with everyone having an appreciation of the others, before the different departments separate to continue work on their particular area of expertise. One may readily imagine how attendance at this crucial first rehearsal will aid the poster designer to produce his own contribution in overall unity with the mood, theme, and atmosphere of the production, as seen by the director. It is only since about 1880 that the modern conception of the director as the principal senior interpreter of the author's work began to gain force. This was in response to drastic changes in the written drama put in motion by the influence of Ibsen, as mentioned earlier. The co-ordinating function of the director was now to oversee all elements of production, and bring them into conformity with his interpretation of the text and/or score.

The philosophy of the modern theatre poster goes well beyond that of the earlier playbill, which was informational only. The poster must now carry an interpretative element, and this must ideally be in harmony with the interpretation of the director. Whether or not the poster designer is also a member of the team in some other capacity, or is present at the first reading, the poster should be consistent with the unity of style which is the first principle of modern play production.

The Broadway theatre poster in the twentieth century, therefore, is seen as depicting the essential theme or story motif of the play, and not merely as a factual advertisement, no matter how visually attractive.

It is hard to conceive of an industry better suited to advertising itself than show business. In modern times, the New York critics became such powerful arbiters of public taste that six or seven men could literally close a production within a week. *The New York Times* critic has traditionally carried the most weight. Fortunately, for a very long time its critic was Brooks Atkinson (b.1894), a man of such fairness and impeccable judgment that a Broadway theatre was later named after him in gratitude. Nevertheless, the situation was and is extreme. Modern posters increasingly depicted key words, or phrases from the reviews were quoted on later editions of the posters, in a manner not unlike the superlatives found on nineteenth-century samples. Through no fault of the modern critic, out-of-context phrases can be highly misleading, and a fair proportion are just that. Mention of any awards which the play might have won would also appear on later editions of the posters, and one can assume that 'later' editions might appear very soon indeed if the box office needed quick stimulus after the opening night.

The poster may well be the first impression which the potential patron forms of a production and is therefore crucially important, especially in the New York context, where plays are so subject to market forces and professional opinion as to register instant failure or instant success. Not having tax subsidy, nor the benefits of a repertory system which can carry a worthy but weak play on the back of the more commercially successful one for a time by alternating performances, the importance of the first impression created by the poster can hardly be exaggerated. The problem of communication which the poster poses for the designer is clearly greater with a totally unknown new play than with a respected play undergoing a revival. But the problem with promoting a revival of something which previously failed, even if worthy, is obviously much greater. The more familiar the poster designer can be with the text and/or score, and even more so with the director's concept, the more likely it is that the poster will produce a positive first impression. Last, but not least, mention must be made of the need for absolute

accuracy on the poster as far as contractual arrangements with actors and other personnel who are to be billed on the poster are concerned. This would also apply to heirs or copyright holders of material used in the production.

The colored posters and black-and-white playbills illustrated on these pages were selected because they advertise productions which were of historical importance from a literary or musical point of view, are representative of a type which was significant, or are of popular or visual interest. These illustrations represent a capsule history of the Broadway stage from 1750 to 1992. The earlier examples content themselves with calling the viewer's attention to the 'who, what, when, and where' of the production. The later examples increasingly reflect the 'why,' which is to say, they address the theme or style of the production.

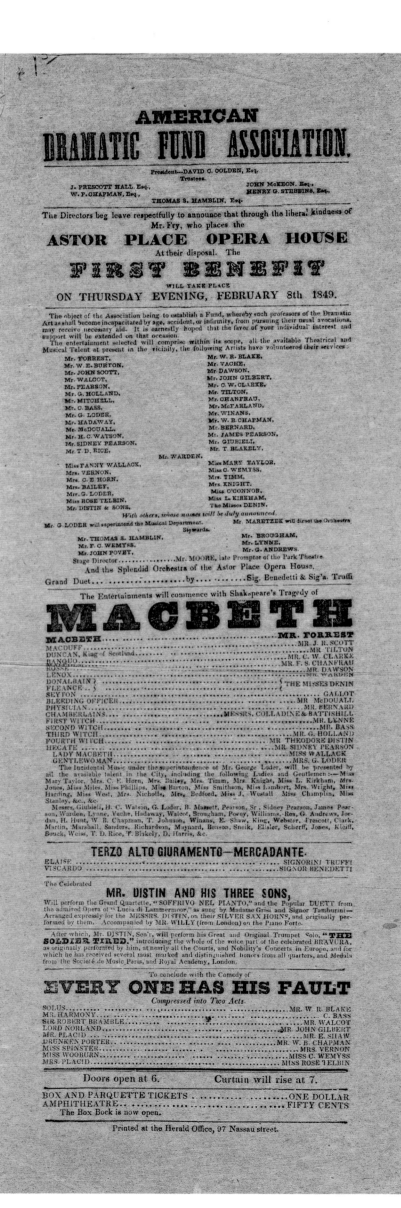

The Black Crook, 1879
Poster
Color lithograph
Courtesy Performing Arts Research Center
The New York Public Library at Lincoln Center

Macbeth, 1849
Poster for the Astor Place Opera House
Letterpress
Theatre Arts Collection, Harry Ransom Humanities
Research Center, The University of Texas at Austin

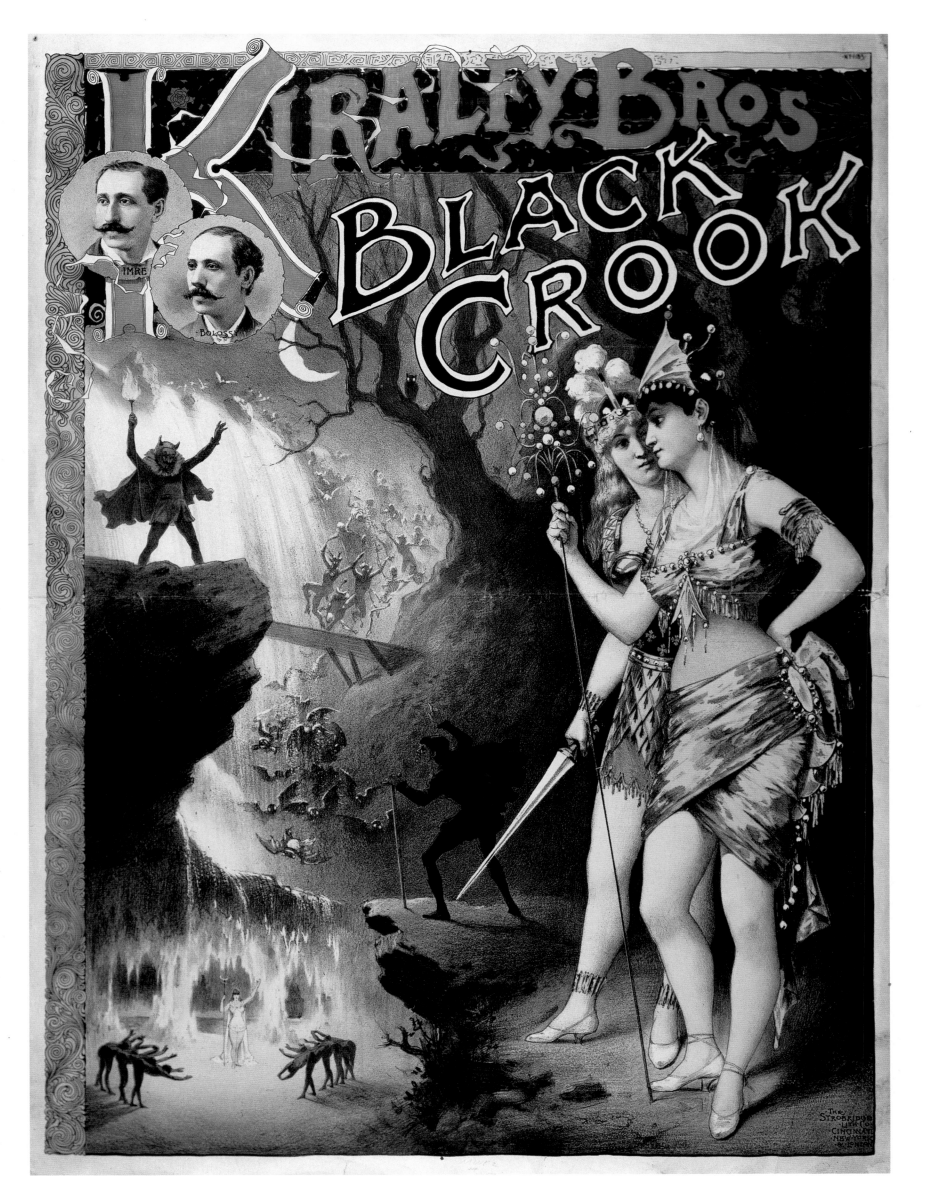

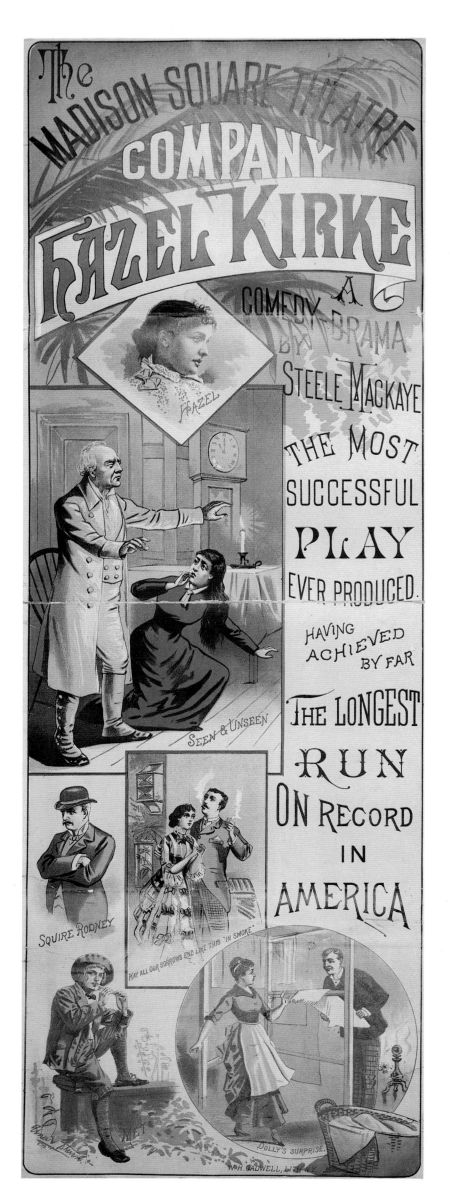

Hazel Kirke, 1880
Poster for the Madison Square Theatre
Color lithograph
Courtesy Performing Arts Research Center
The New York Public Library,
at Lincoln Center

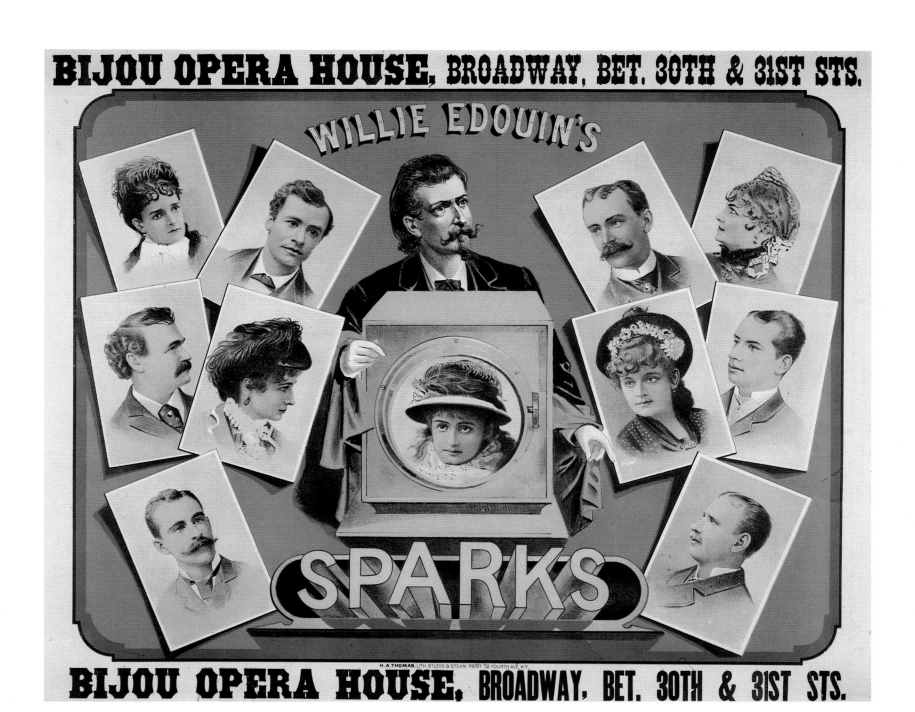

Willie Edouin's Sparks Company, 1882
Poster
Color lithograph
Courtesy The Antique Poster Collection Gallery,
Ridgefield, CT, a division of George J Goodstadt, Inc

Little Lord Fauntleroy, 1888
Poster
Color lithograph
Poster Collection, Theatre Arts Collection, Harry
Ransom Humanities Research Center, The University
of Texas at Austin

The Mascot, 1882
Poster for the Germania Theater
Color lithograph
Courtesy The Antique Poster Collection Gallery,
Ridgefield, CT, a division of George J Goodstadt, Inc

Shenandoah, 1889
Poster
Color lithograph
Courtesy The Antique Poster Collection Gallery,
Ridgefield, CT, a division of George J Goodstadt, Inc

The Heroines of Shenandoah, 1889
Poster for the Grand Opera House
Color lithograph
Poster Collection, Theatre Arts Collection, Harry
Ransom Humanities Research Center, The University
of Texas at Austin

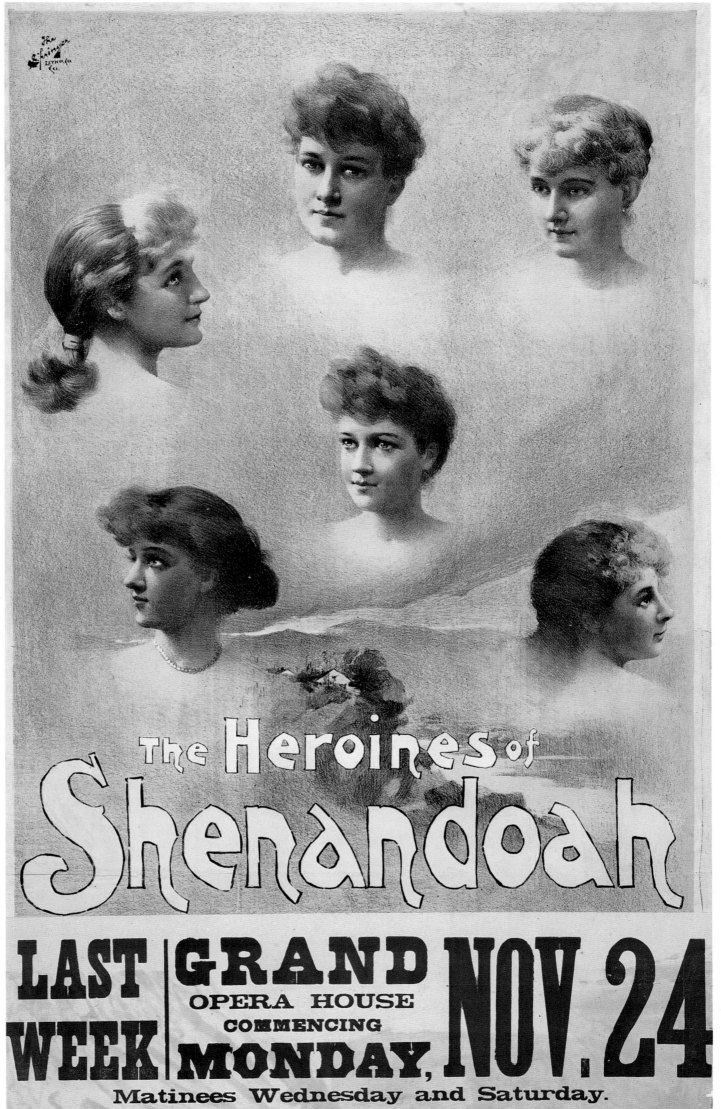

THE CHARITY BALL

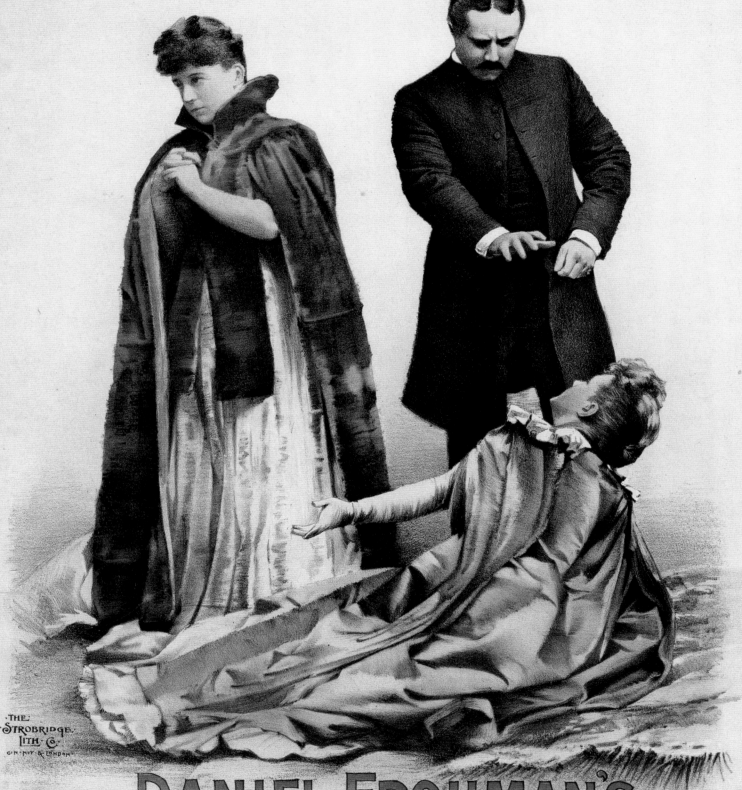

DANIEL FROHMAN'S
LYCEUM THEATRE SUCCESS.
Written by BELASCO & DE MILLE.

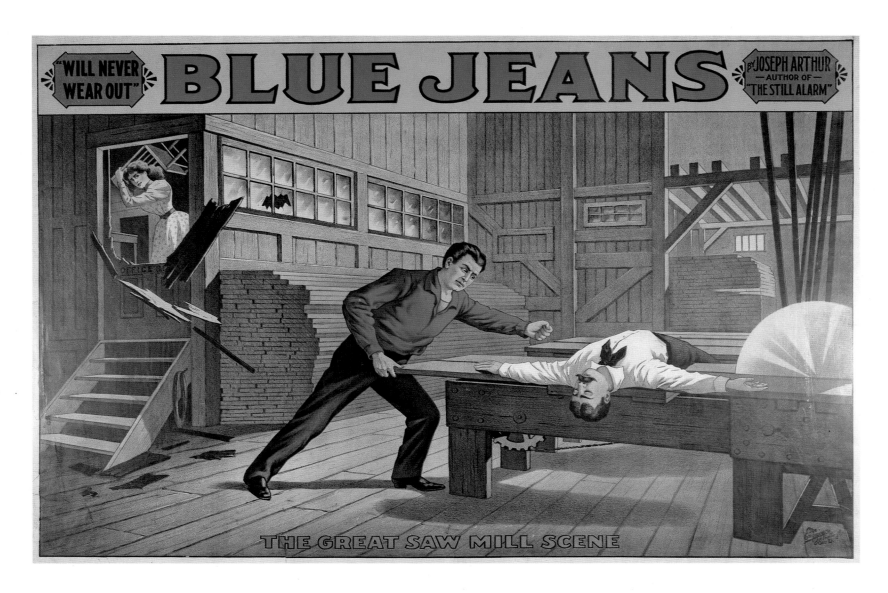

Blue Jeans, 1891
Poster
Color lithograph
Courtesy The Antique Poster Collection Gallery,
Ridgefield, CT, a division of George J Goodstadt, Inc

The Charity Ball, 1889
Poster for the Lyceum Theater
Color lithograph
Courtesy The Antique Poster Collection Gallery,
Ridgefield, CT, a division of George J Goodstadt, Inc

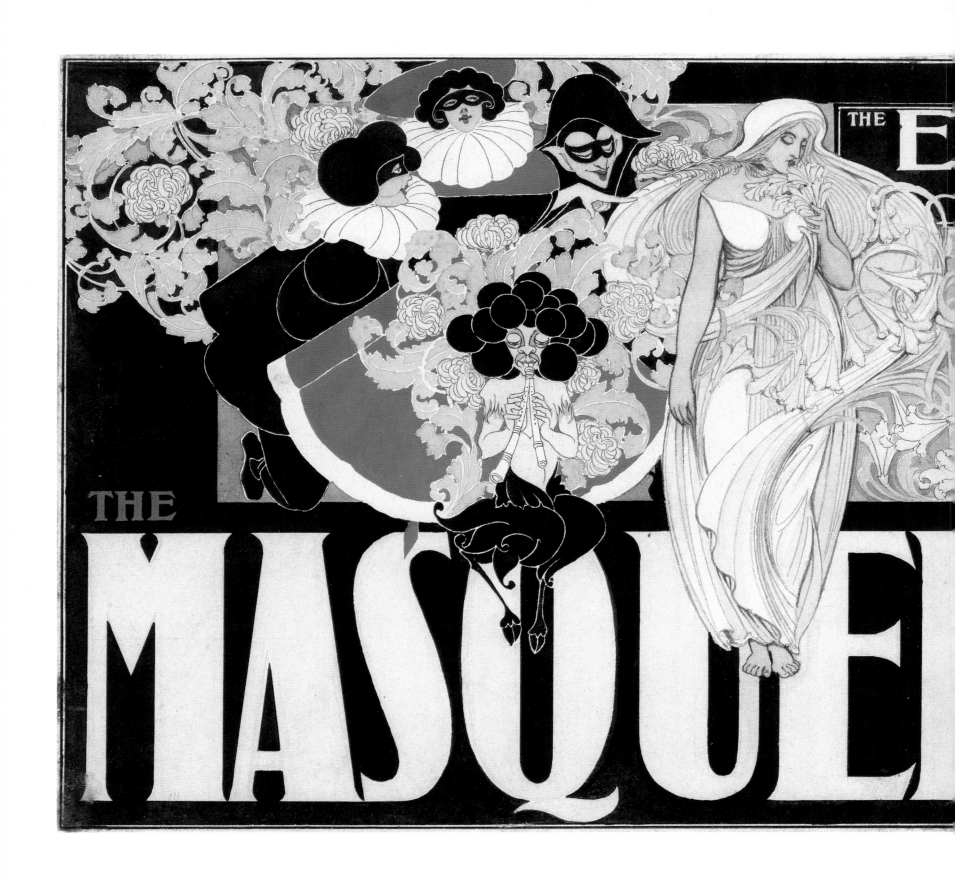

The Masqueraders, 1894
Poster designed by Will H Bradley
Pencil, pen and ink on paper, 8½ × 19¼ inches (21.8 × 49.3 cm)
The Metropolitan Museum of Art
Gift of Fern Bradley Dufner, 1952 (52.625.143)

MPIRE THEATRE COMPANY
NEW YORK
IN HENRY ARTHUR JONES COMEDY
RADERS

Bohemia, 1895
Poster for the Empire Theatre
Color lithograph
Courtesy The Antique Poster Collection Gallery,
Ridgefield, CT, a division of George J Goodstadt, Inc

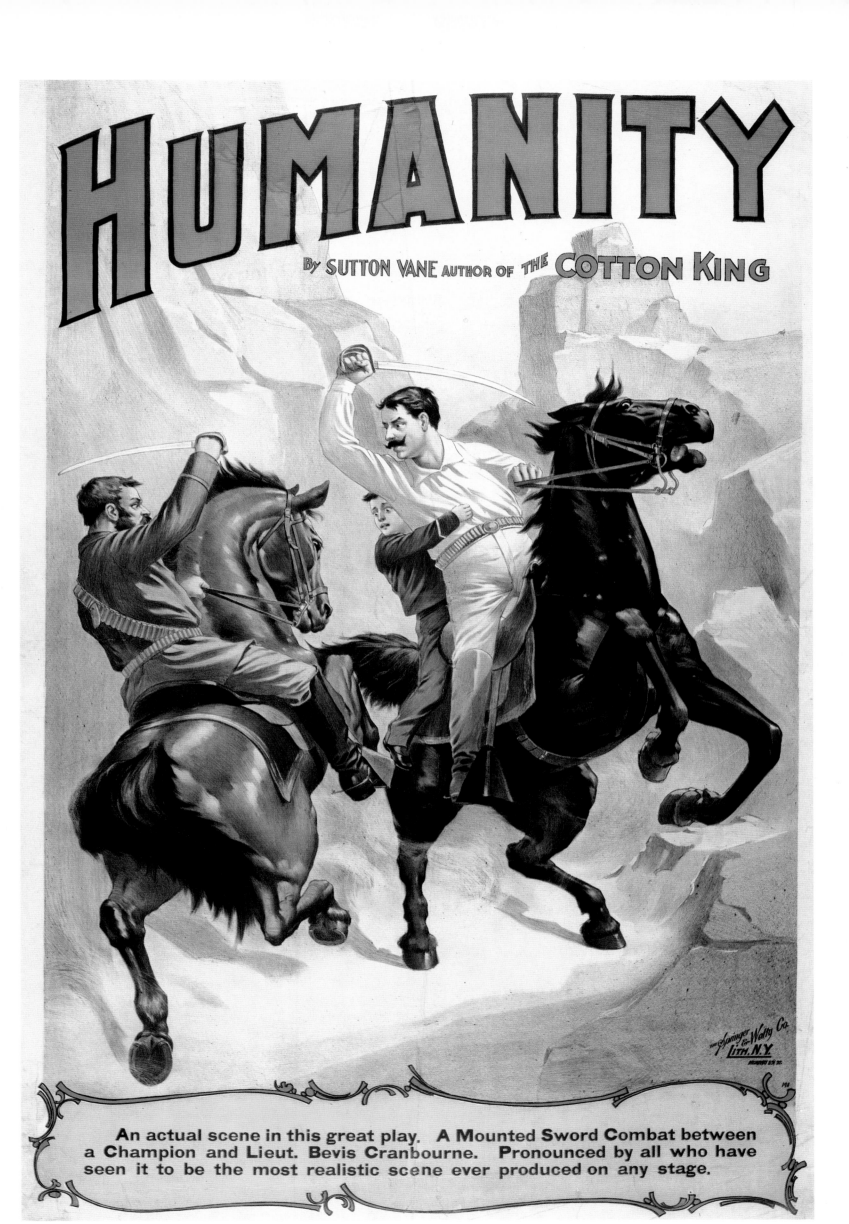

HUMANITY

BY SUTTON VANE AUTHOR OF THE COTTON KING

An actual scene in this great play. A Mounted Sword Combat between a Champion and Lieut. Bevis Cranbourne. Pronounced by all who have seen it to be the most realistic scene ever produced on any stage.

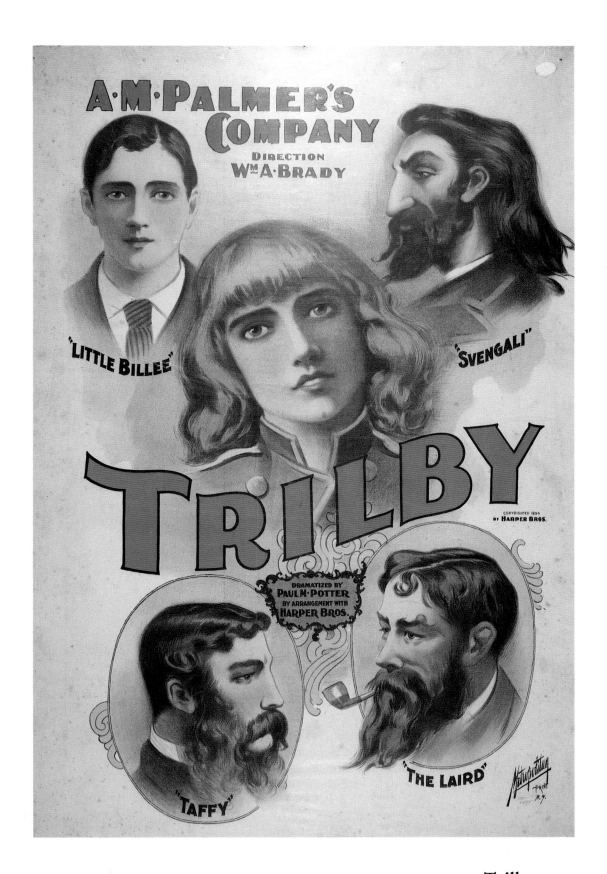

Trilby, 1896
Poster
Color lithograph
Courtesy The Antique Poster Collection Gallery,
Ridgefield, CT, a division of George J Goodstadt, Inc

El Capitan, 1896
Poster
Color lithograph
Courtesy The Antique Poster Collection Gallery,
Ridgefield, CT, a division of George J Goodstadt, Inc

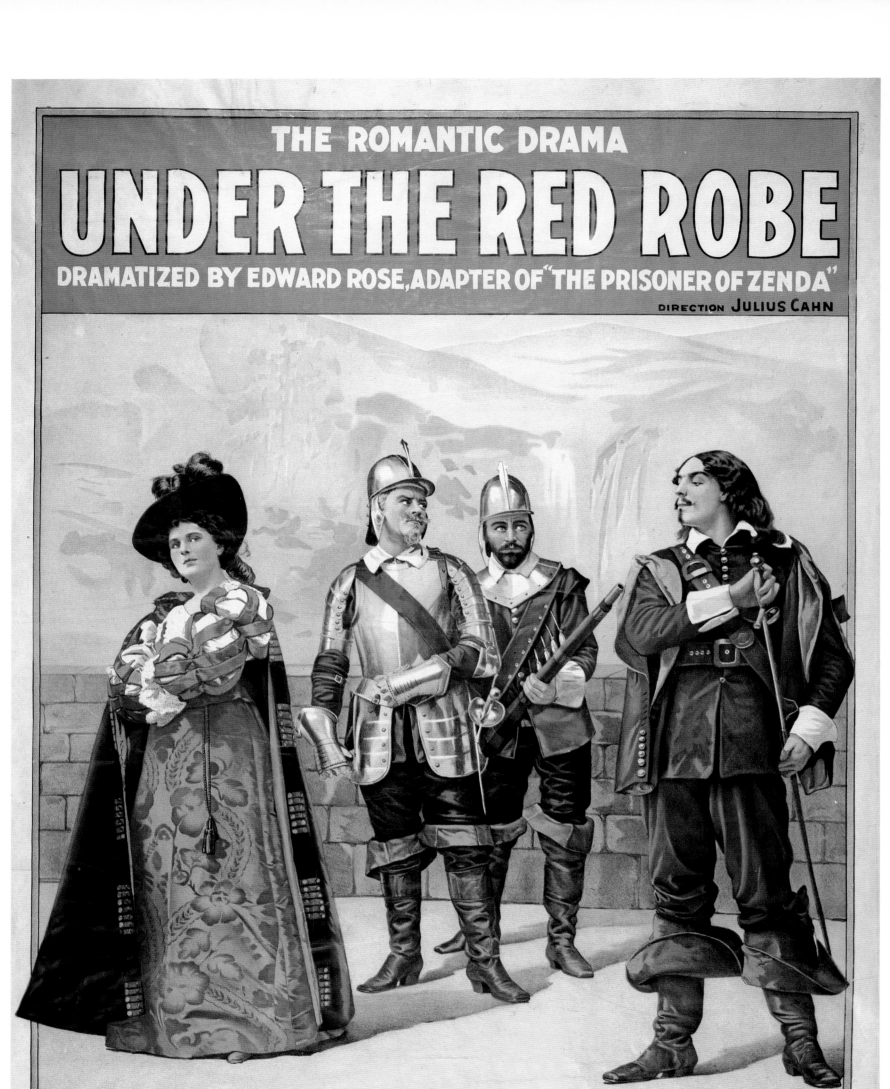

THE ROMANTIC DRAMA

UNDER THE RED ROBE

DRAMATIZED BY EDWARD ROSE, ADAPTER OF "THE PRISONER OF ZENDA"

DIRECTION JULIUS CAHN

"SHE WILL HEAR IT FROM HIM."

Otis Skinner as Romeo, 1896
Poster
Color lithograph
Courtesy The Antique Poster Collection Gallery,
Ridgefield, CT, a division of George J Goodstadt, Inc

Under the Red Robe, 1896
Poster
Color lithograph
Courtesy The Antique Poster Collection Gallery,
Ridgefield, CT, a division of George J Goodstadt, Inc

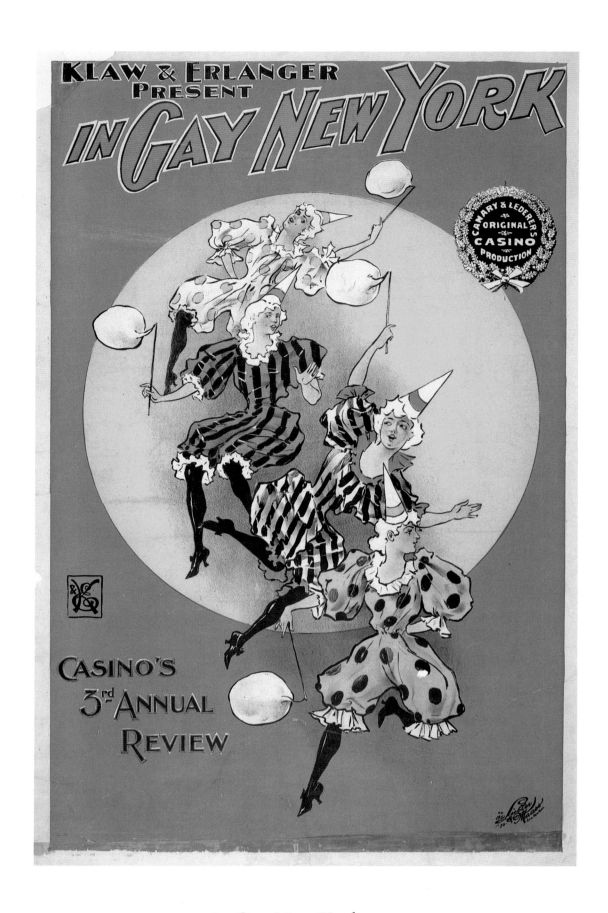

In Gay New York, 1898
Poster
Color lithograph
Courtesy The Antique Poster Collection Gallery,
Ridgefield, CT, a division of George J Goodstadt, Inc

The Pride of Jennico, 1900
Poster
Color lithograph
Courtesy The Antique Poster Collection Gallery,
Ridgefield, CT, a division of George J Goodstadt, Inc

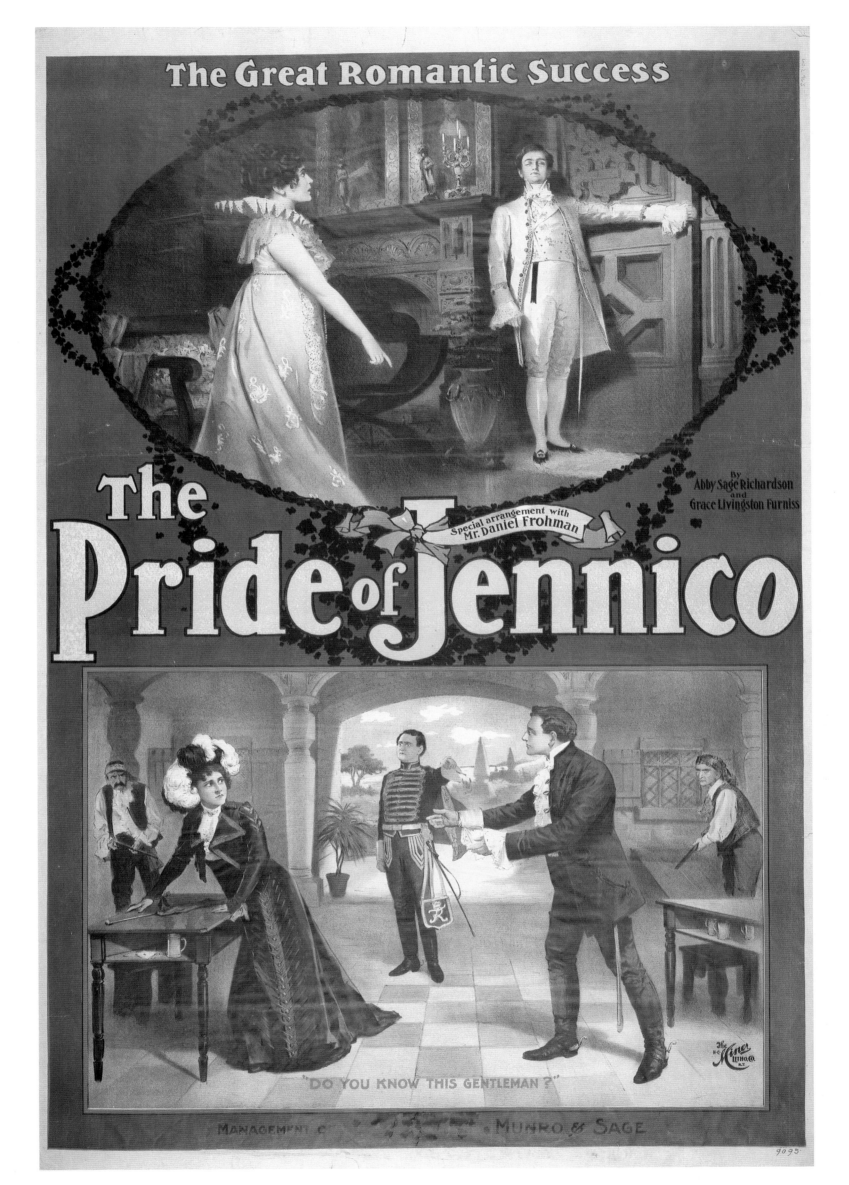

The Great Romantic Success

The **Pride** of **Jennico**

Special arrangement with Mr. Daniel Frohman

By Abby Sage Richardson and Grace Livingston Furniss

"DO YOU KNOW THIS GENTLEMAN?"

MANAGEMENT OF MUNRO & SAGE

A Modern Cinderella, c. 1900
Poster
Color lithograph
Courtesy The Antique Poster Collection
Gallery, Ridgefield, CT, a division of
George J Goodstadt, Inc

Prince of Pilsen, 1903
Poster
Color lithograph
Courtesy The Antique Poster Collection Gallery,
Ridgefield, CT, a division of George J Goodstadt, Inc

The Wizard of Oz, 1903
Poster
Color lithograph
Museum of the City of New York, The Theater Collection

Peter Pan, 1905
Window card for the Empire Theatre
(photo on cardboard)
*Museum of the City of New York
The Theater Collection*

Kassa, 1909
Poster by Alphonse Mucha
Poster Collection
*Theatre Arts Collection, Harry Ransom Humanities
Research Center, The University of Texas at Austin*

The White Slave, 1911
Poster
Color lithograph
*Courtesy The Antique Poster Collection Gallery,
Ridgefield, CT, a division of George J Goodstadt, Inc*

Maude Adams as Joan of Arc, 1909
Poster designed by Alphonse Mucha
Oil on canvas, 82¼ × 30 inches (208.9 × 76.2 cm)
*The Metropolitan Museum of Art
Gift of A J Kobler, 1920 (20.33)*

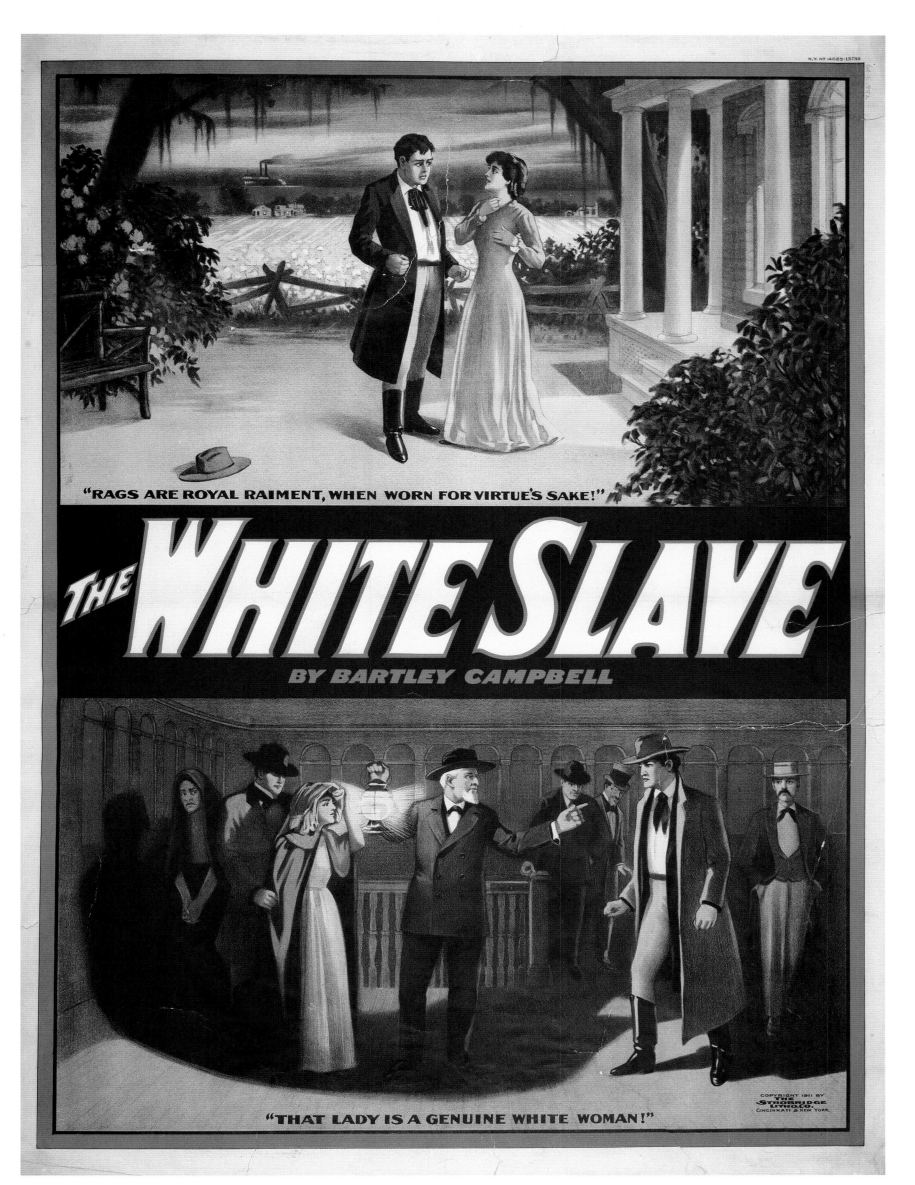

N.Y. № 14368
THE BIGGEST COMEDY SUCCESS OF THE DECADE
Peg o' My Heart
BY J. HARTLEY MANNERS
COPYRIGHT 1913 BY
THE STROBRIDGE LITHO. CO.
CINCINNATI & NEW YORK
ETHEL! — "PLEASE DONT: IT'S SO HOT THIS MORNING!"

Caesar and Cleopatra, 1925
Window card for the Theatre Guild
Designed by Gil Spear
The Beinecke Rare Book and Manuscript Library
Yale University

Peg o' My Heart, 1912
Poster
Color lithograph
Courtesy of the New-York Historical Society, NYC

The Silver Cord, 1926
Window card for the Theatre Guild
Designed by Gil Spear
The Beinecke Rare Book and Manuscript Library
Yale University

Juarez and Maximilian, 1926
Window card for the Theatre Guild
Designed by Gil Spear
The Beinecke Rare Book and Manuscript Library
Yale University

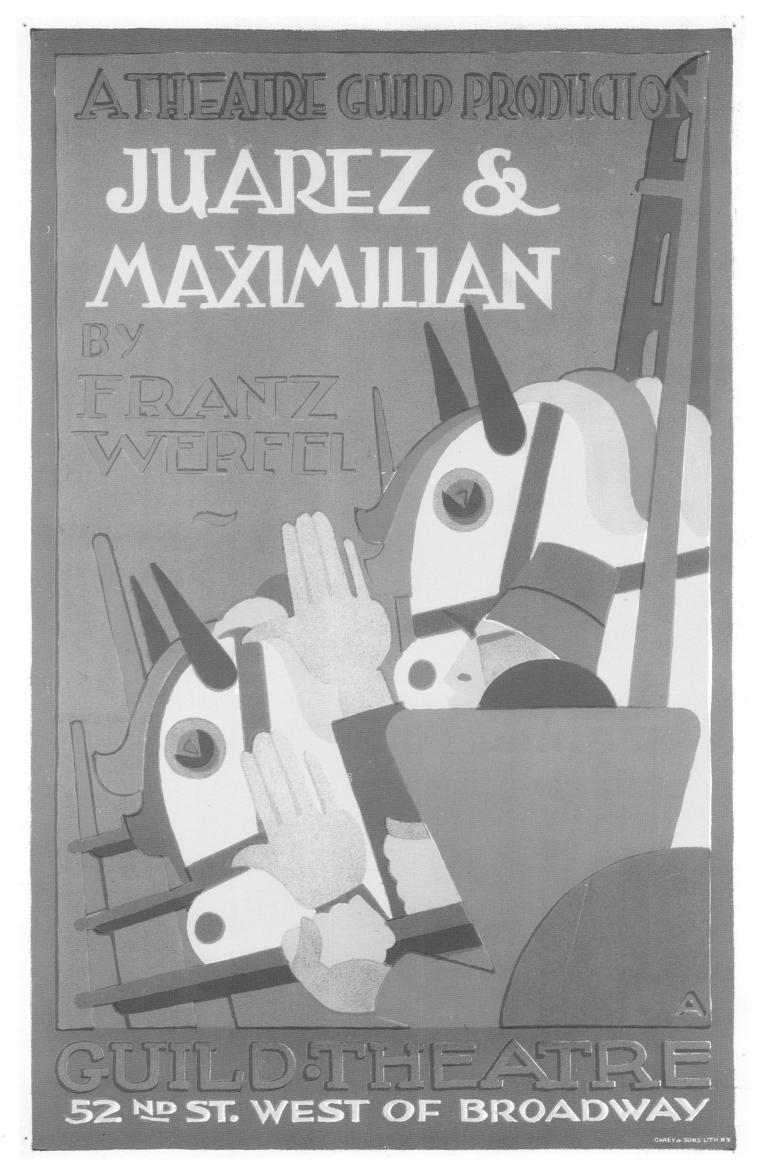

Porgy, 1927
Window card for the Theatre Guild
Designed by Lee Simonson
The Beinecke Rare Book and Manuscript Library
Yale University

Major Barbara, 1928
Window card for the Theatre Guild
Designed by Carroll C Snell
The Beinecke Rare Book and Manuscript Library
Yale University

Strange Interlude, 1928
Window card for the Theatre Guild
*Museum of the City of New York, The Theater
Collection*

Marco Millions, 1928
Window card for the Theatre Guild
Designed by Lee Simonson
*Courtesy Performing Arts Research Center
The New York Public Library at Lincoln Center*

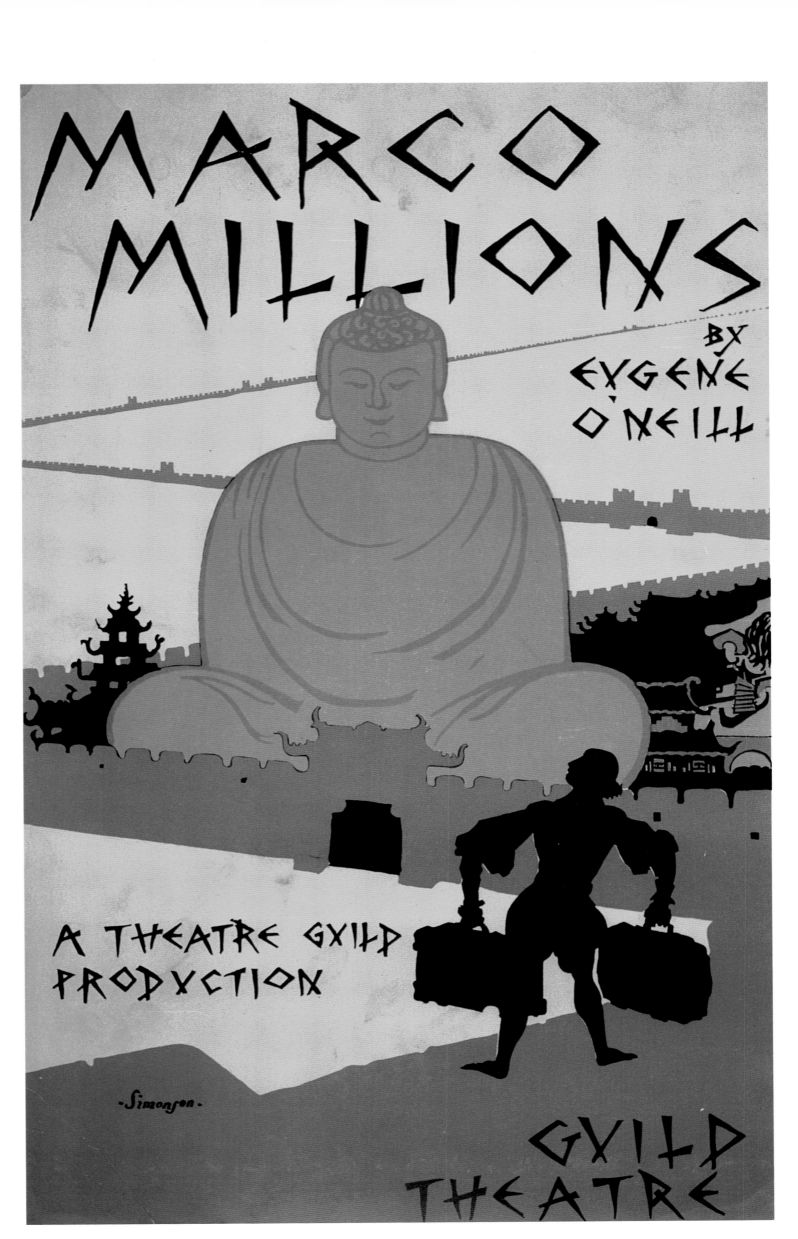

MARCO MILLIONS

BY EYGENE O'NEILL

A THEATRE GYILD PRODYCTION

Simonson

GYILD THEATRE

Journey's End, 1929
Window card
Museum of the City of New York, The Theater Collection

The Green Pastures, 1930
Window card
Courtesy of The Performing Arts Research Center
The New York Picture Library at Lincoln Center

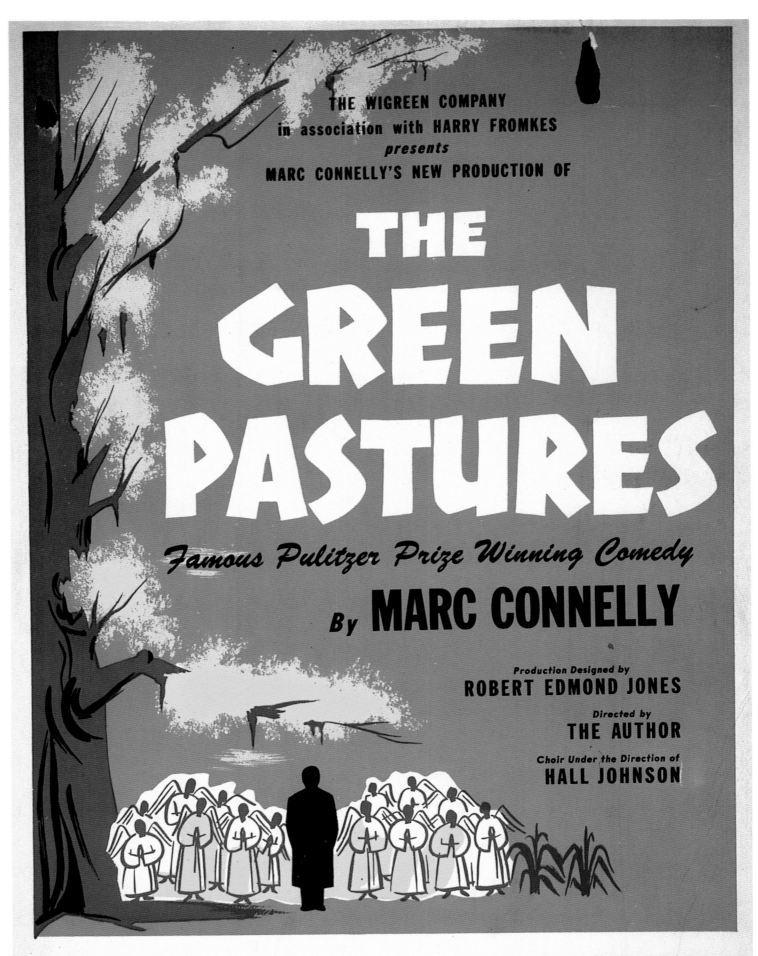

THE WIGREEN COMPANY
in association with HARRY FROMKES
presents
MARC CONNELLY'S NEW PRODUCTION OF

THE GREEN PASTURES

Famous Pulitzer Prize Winning Comedy

By **MARC CONNELLY**

Production Designed by
ROBERT EDMOND JONES

Directed by
THE AUTHOR

Choir Under the Direction of
HALL JOHNSON

BROADWAY THEATRE

BROADWAY AT 53rd STREET

MATINEES WEDNESDAY AND SATURDAY

THE THEATRE GUILD
PRESENTS

MOURNING BECOMES ELECTRA
A TRILOGY BY EUGENE O'NEILL

1st PLAY . HOMECOMING
2nd PLAY . THE HUNTED
3rd PLAY . THE HAUNTED

GUILD THEATRE
52nd ST. WEST OF BROADWAY

D. SHERWOOD

Biography, 1932
Window card for the Theatre Guild
Designed by D Sherwood
The Beinecke Rare Book and Manuscript Library
Yale University

Mourning Becomes Electra, 1931
Window card for the Theatre Guild
Designed by D Sherwood
The Beinecke Rare Book and Manuscript Library
Yale University

Too True to be Good, 1932
Window card for the Theatre Guild
Designed by F M Walts
Courtesy Performing Arts Research Center
The New York Public Library Lincoln Center

Mary of Scotland, 1933
Window card for the Theatre Guild
Designed by Massaguer
The Beinecke Rare Book and Manuscript Library
Yale University

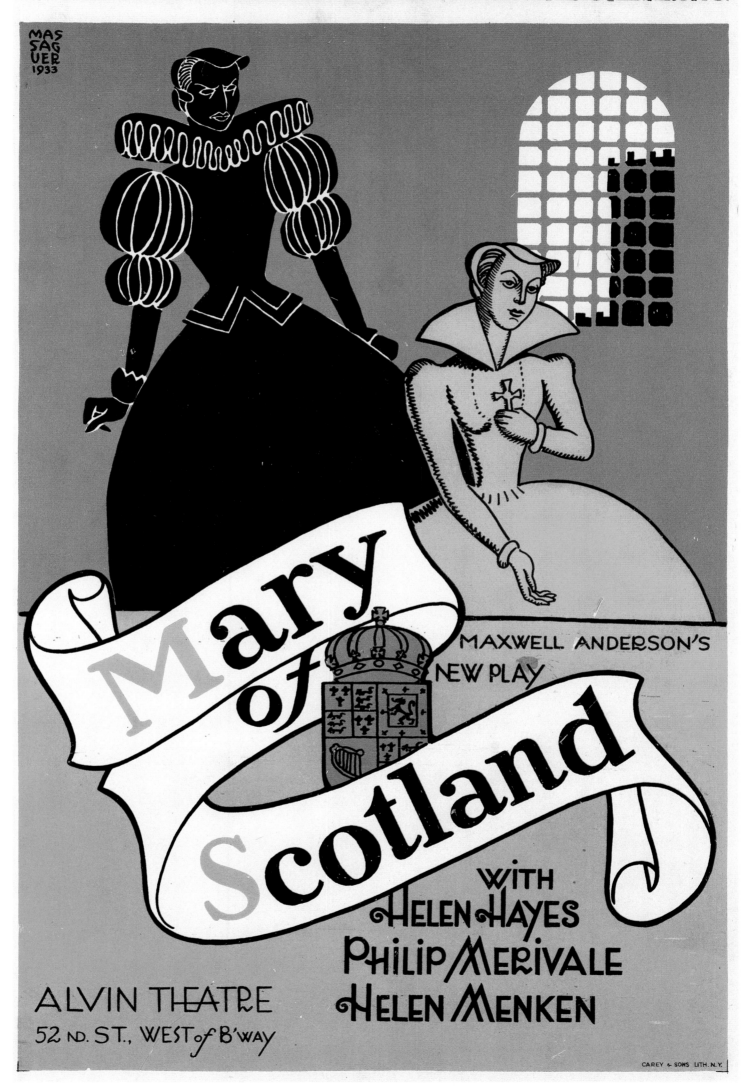

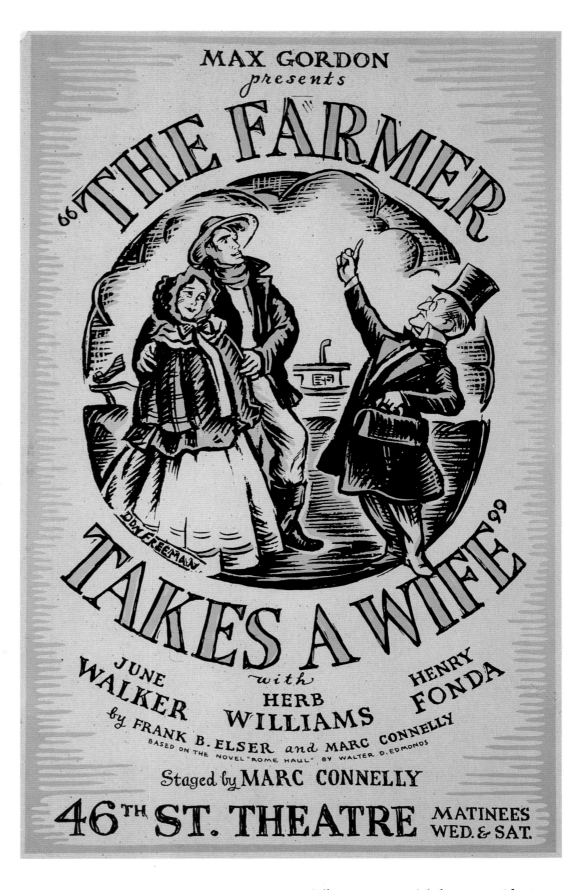

The Farmer Takes a Wife, 1934
Window card
*Museum of the City of New York, The Theater
Collection*

Roberta, 1933
Window card
*Museum of the City of New York, The Theater
Collection*

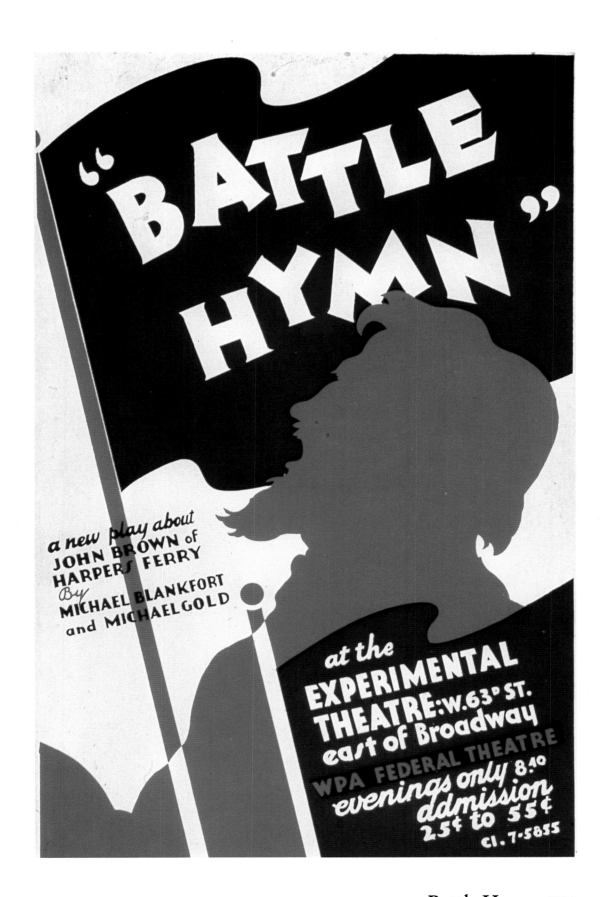

Battle Hymn, 1936
WPA Poster for the Federal Theater Project
George Mason University, Fairfax, VA

Jumbo, 1935
Window card
*Museum of the City of New York, The Theater
Collection*

Horse Eats Hat, 1936
WPA Poster for the Federal Theater Project
George Mason University, Fairfax, VA

Idiot's Delight, 1936
Window card
*Museum of the City of New York, The Theater
Collection*

Federal Theatre
presents

GEORGE BERNARD SHAW'S
ANDROCLES AND THE LION
A NEGRO PRODUCTION

Halls

LAFAYETTE
THEATRE
132nd STREET · 7th AVENUE

MADE BY WPA FEDERAL ART PROJECT NYC

Power, 1937
WPA Poster for the Federal Theater Project
George Mason University, Fairfax, VA

Androcles and the Lion, 1937
WPA Poster for the Federal Theater Project
George Mason University, Fairfax, VA

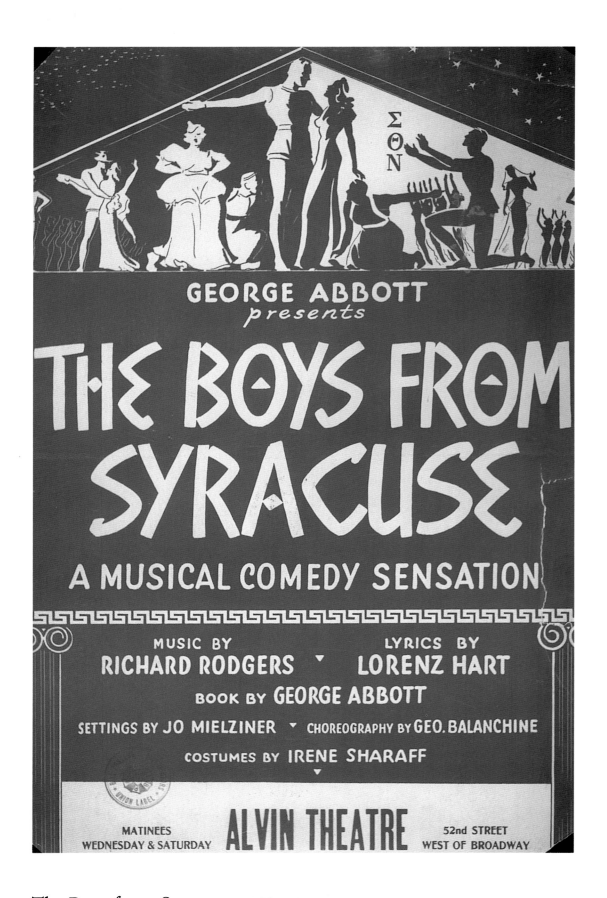

The Boys from Syracuse, 1938
Window card
Courtesy Performing Arts Research Center
The New York Public Library at Lincoln Center

The Philadelphia Story, 1939
Window card design for the Theatre Guild
The Beinecke Rare Book and Manuscript Library
Yale University

The THEATRE GUILD
presents
A NEW COMEDY BY
PHILIP BARRY

The PHILADELPHIA STORY

WITH

KATHARINE HEPBURN

VAN HEFLIN   JOSEPH COTTEN   NICHOLAS JOY

DIRECTED BY ROBERT B. SINCLAIR

SETTINGS DESIGNED AND LIGHTED BY
ROBERT EDMOND JONES

PRODUCED UNDER THE SUPERVISION OF
THERESA HELBURN & LAWRENCE LANGNER

SHUBERT THEATRE
44th St. West of Broadway

The Theatre Guild & Gilbert Miller present

HELEN HAYES · MAURICE EVANS

in William Shakespeare's Comedy

· TWELFTH NIGHT ·

with
JUNE WALKER · SOPHIE STEWART · DONALD BURR · MARK SMITH

Directed by MARGARET WEBSTER

SETTINGS & COSTUMES by STEWART CHANEY   MUSIC by PAUL BOWLES

PRODUCTION UNDER THE SUPERVISION OF THERESA HELBURN & LAWRENCE LANGNER

ST. JAMES THEATRE

44TH ST. W OF B'WAY   -   MATS. THURS. & SAT.

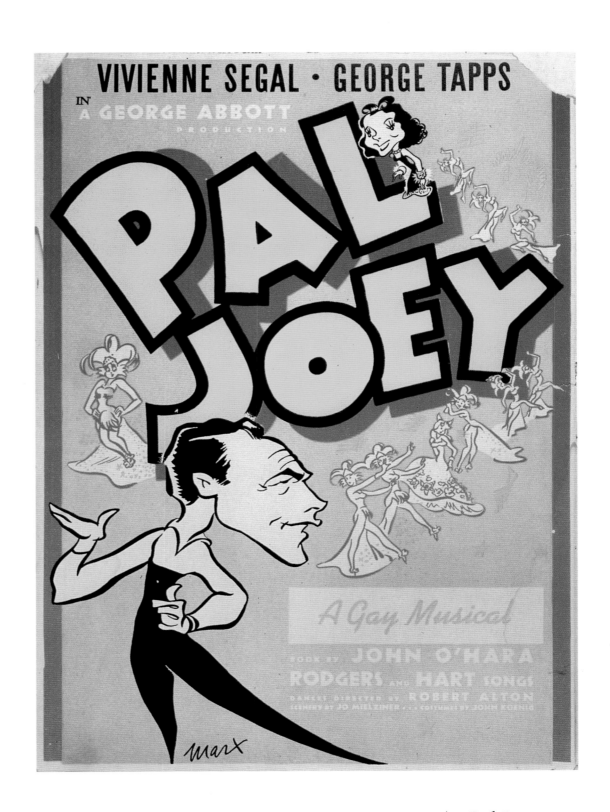

Pal Joey, 1940
Window card
Courtesy Performing Arts Research Center
The New York Public Library at Lincoln Center

Twelfth Night, 1940
Window card
*Museum of the City of New York, The Theater
Collection*

"JUST THE PLACE TO DIE LAUGHING" JOHN ANDERSON —JOURNAL AMERICAN

JOHN C. WILSON
PRESENTS

DENNIS ESTELLE CAROL
KING ANNABELLA WINWOOD GOODNER
IN
BLITHE SPIRIT
THE COMEDY HIT BY
NOEL COWARD
STAGED BY Mr. WILSON   SETTING BY STEWART CHANEY

Blithe Spirit, 1941
Window card
Museum of the City of New York, The Theater
Collection

The Skin of our Teeth, 1942
Window card designed by Don Freeman
Courtesy Performing Arts Research Center
The New York Public Library at Lincoln Center

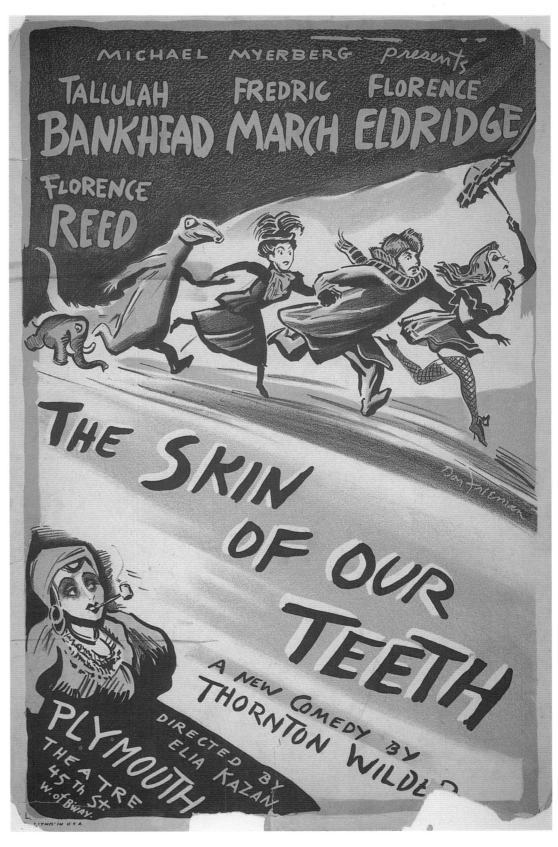

This is the Army, 1942
Window card
Courtesy Performing Arts Research Center
The New York Public Library at Lincoln Center

Oklahoma!, 1943
Window card
Museum of the City of New York, The Theater
Collection

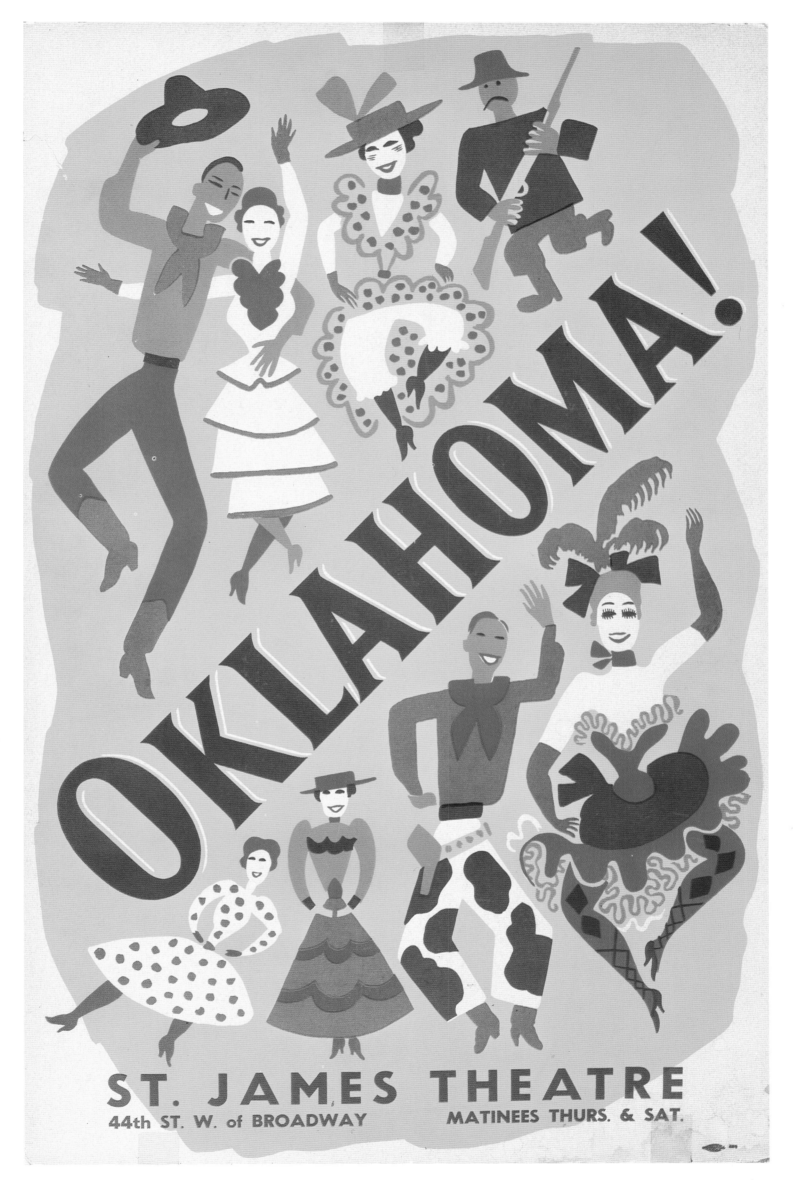

OKLAHOMA!

ST. JAMES THEATRE

44th ST. W. of BROADWAY   MATINEES THURS. & SAT.

Helen Goes to Troy, 1944
Window card designed by Al Hirschfeld
Courtesy Performing Arts Research Center
The New York Public Library at Lincoln Center

Carousel, 1945
Window card for the Theatre Guild
The Beinecke Rare Book and Manuscript Library
Yale University

THE THEATRE GUILD presents

Carousel

(Based on FERENC MOLNAR'S "LILIOM" as adapted by Benjamin F. Glazer)

"IT'S A SMASH HIT" —MOREHOUSE. Sun

Music by RICHARD RODGERS
Book and Lyrics by OSCAR HAMMERSTEIN 2d
Directed by ROUBEN MAMOULIAN
Dances by AGNES DE MILLE
Settings by JO MIELZINER
Costumes by MILES WHITE

"ONE OF THE FINEST MUSICAL PLAYS I HAVE EVER SEEN."
—JOHN CHAPMAN, N.Y. Daily News

★ Production Supervised by LAWRENCE LANGNER and THERESA HELBURN ★

MAJESTIC THEATRE

44th STREET WEST OF BROADWAY   MATS. THURS. & SAT.

491

Annie Get Your Gun, 1946
Window card
Courtesy Performing Arts Research Center
The New York Public Library at Lincoln Center

The Iceman Cometh, 1946
Window card
Courtesy Performing Arts Research Center
The New York Public Library at Lincoln Center

The Theatre Guild

presents

EUGENE O'NEILL'S

"The Iceman Cometh"

JAMES BARTON   **DUDLEY DIGGES**

CARL BENTON REID   **NICHOLAS JOY**

Directed by **EDDIE DOWLING**

Production designed and lighted by **ROBERT EDMOND JONES**

Production under the supervision of
THERESA HELBURN and **LAWRENCE LANGNER**

Associate Producer **Armina Marshall**

MARTIN BECK THEATRE

45th ST. W. of 8th AVE.   Curtain at 7:30 Sharp
Eves. only, TUES. THRU SUN.   •   (No Perf. Mon.)

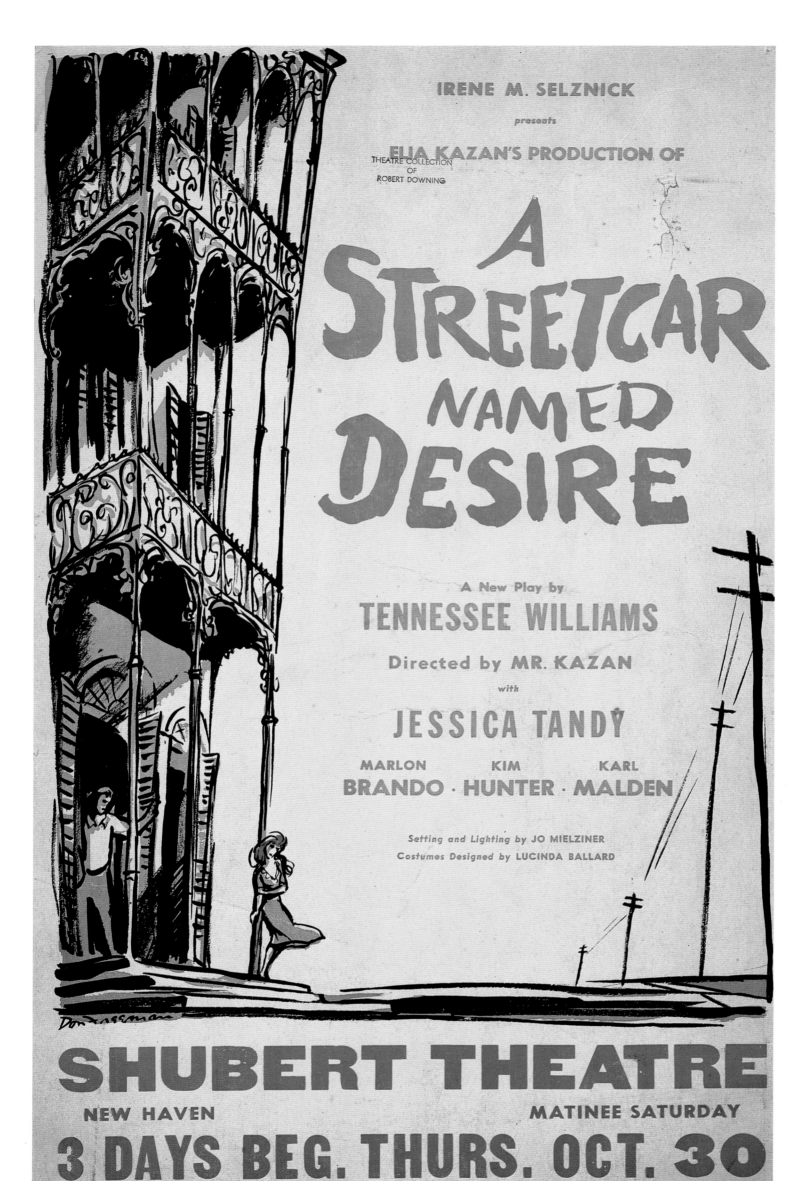

IRENE M. SELZNICK

presents

ELIA KAZAN'S PRODUCTION OF

THEATRE COLLECTION
OF
ROBERT DOWNING

A STREETCAR NAMED DESIRE

A New Play by
TENNESSEE WILLIAMS

Directed by MR. KAZAN

with

JESSICA TANDY

MARLON   KIM   KARL
BRANDO · HUNTER · MALDEN

Setting and Lighting by JO MIELZINER
Costumes Designed by LUCINDA BALLARD

SHUBERT THEATRE

NEW HAVEN   MATINEE SATURDAY

3 DAYS BEG. THURS. OCT. 30

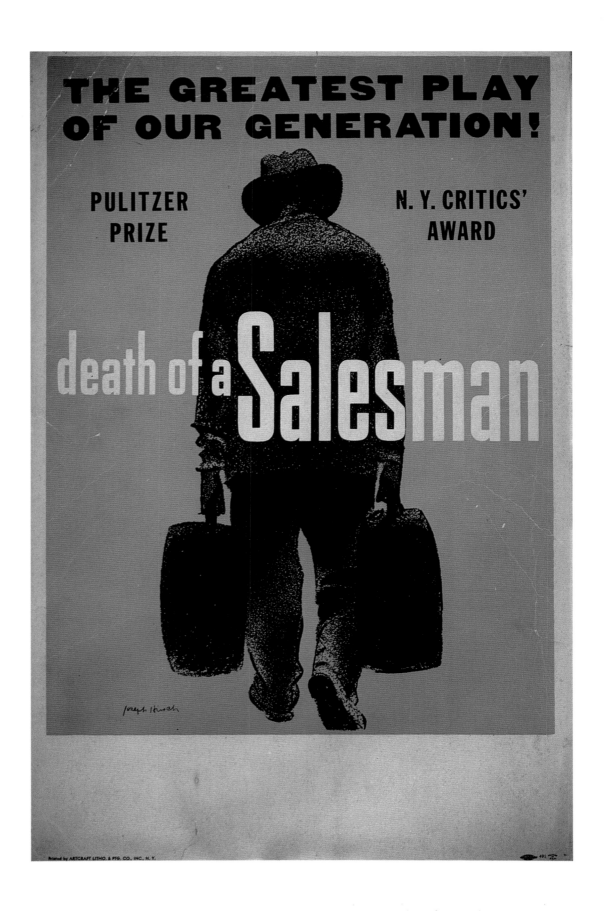

Death of a Salesman, 1949
Window card
Courtesy Performing Arts Research Center
The New York Public Library at Lincoln Center

A Streetcar Named Desire, 1947
Poster
Robert Downing Collection
Theatre Arts Collection, Harry Ransom Humanities
Research Center, The University of Texas at Austin

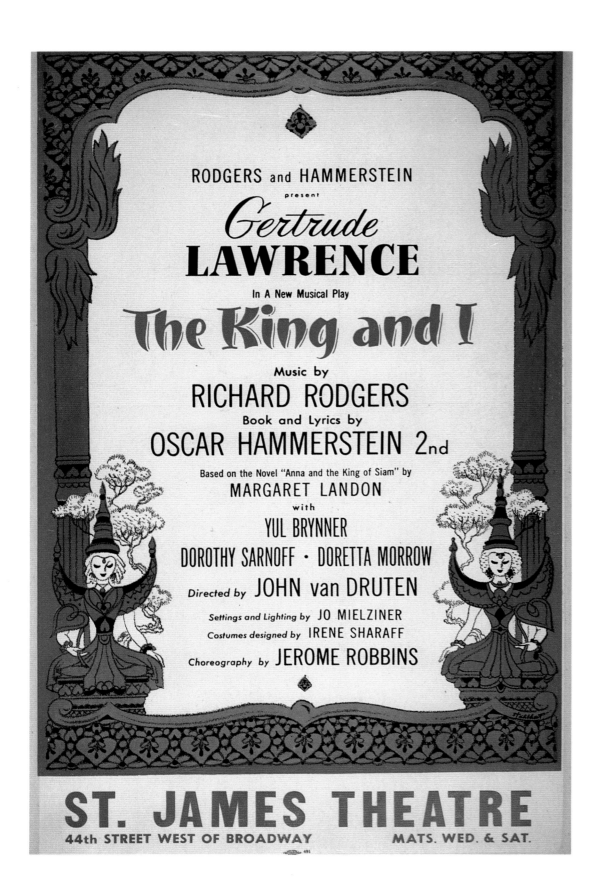

The King and I, 1951
Window card
Courtesy Performing Arts Research Center
The New York Public Library at Lincoln Center

House of Flowers, 1954
Window card
Courtesy Performing Arts Research Center
The New York Public Library at Lincoln Center

SAINT SUBBER presents

TRUMAN CAPOTE and HAROLD ARLEN'S new musical

House of Flowers

starring PEARL BAILEY

direction
PETER BROOK

sets and costumes
OLIVER MESSEL

choreography
GEORGE BALANCHINE

with
| DIAHANN | JUANITA | JOSEPHINE | DINO | RAWN | JACQUES | GEOFFREY |
| **CARROLL** | **HALL** | **PREMICE** | **DiLUCA** | **SPEARMAN** | **AUBUCHON** | **HOLDER** |

and **FREDERICK O'NEAL**

musical director JERRY ARLEN   lighting JEAN ROSENTHAL   orchestrations TED ROYAL

ALVIN THEATRE
52nd ST. W. of B'WAY   MATS. WED. & SAT.

Printed by Artcraft Litho & Ptg. Co. Inc., N. Y. C.

A Cat on a Hot Tin Roof, 1955
Poster
Robert Downing Collection
Theatre Arts Collection, Harry Ransom Humanities
Research Center, The University of Texas at Austin

Long Day's Journey into Night, 1956
Window card
Courtesy Performing Arts Research Center
The New York Public Library at Lincoln Center

A Raisin in the Sun, 1959
Window card
*Museum of the City of New York, The Theater
Collection*

My Fair Lady, 1956
Window card
Designed by Al Hirschfeld
*Museum of the City of New York, The Theater
Collection*

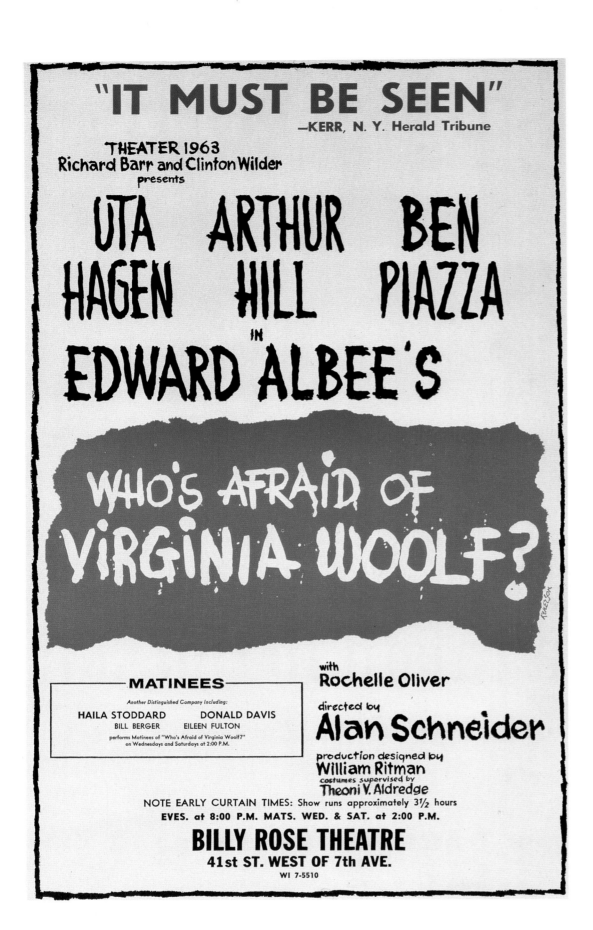

Who's Afraid of Virginia Woolf?, 1962
Window card
*Museum of the City of New York, The Theater
Collection*

Fiddler on the Roof, 1964
Window card
Private Collection

Nederlander Productions, Inc., The Shubert Organization
and the John F. Kennedy Center for The Performing Arts
in association with Theatre Now, Inc.

present

Zero Mostel

in

Fiddler on the Roof
A MUSICAL

Book by **JOSEPH STEIN**
(Based on Sholom Aleichem's stories by special permisson of Arnold Perl)

Music by **JERRY BOCK**

Lyrics by **SHELDON HARNICK**

Direction Reproduced by   Choreography Reproduced by
RUTH MITCHELL   **TOMMY ABBOTT**

Original Direction & Choreography by
JEROME ROBBINS

Settings by   Costumes by   Lighting by
BORIS ARONSON   **PATRICIA ZIPPRODT**   **KEN BILLINGTON**

Orchestrations by   Vocal Arrangements by   Dance Music Arranged by
DON WALKER   **MILTON GREENE**   **BETTY WALBERG**

Originally Produced by **HAROLD PRINCE**

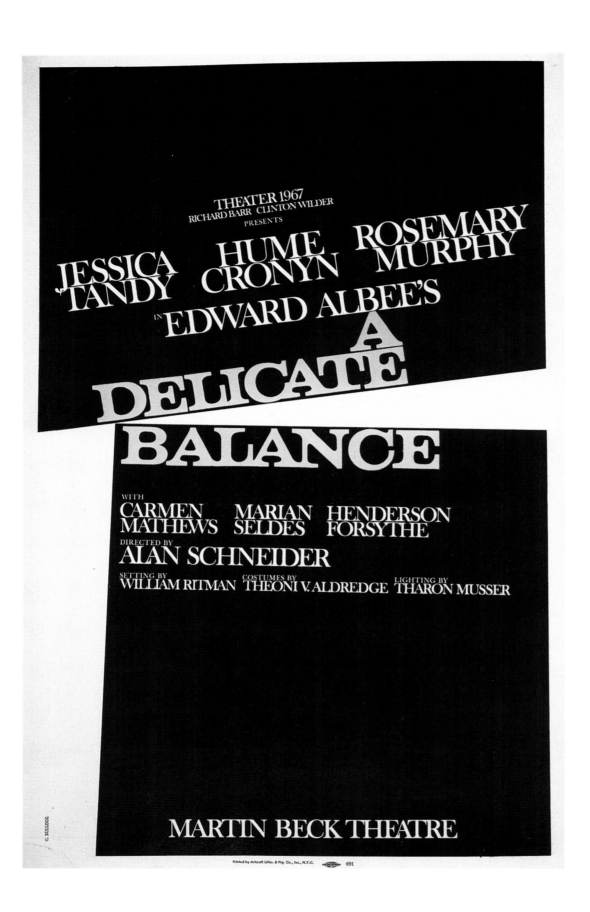

A Delicate Balance, 1966
Window card
Courtesy Performing Arts Research Center
The New York Public Library at Lincoln Center

The Fantasticks, (ninth year) 1969
Poster
W H Crain Collection
Theatre Arts Collection, Harry Ransom Humanities
Research Center, The University of Texas at Austin

181 Sullivan / OR 4-3838

Follies, 1971
Window card
Courtesy Performing Arts Research Center
The New York Public Library at Lincoln Center

Godspell, 1971
Window card
Private Collection

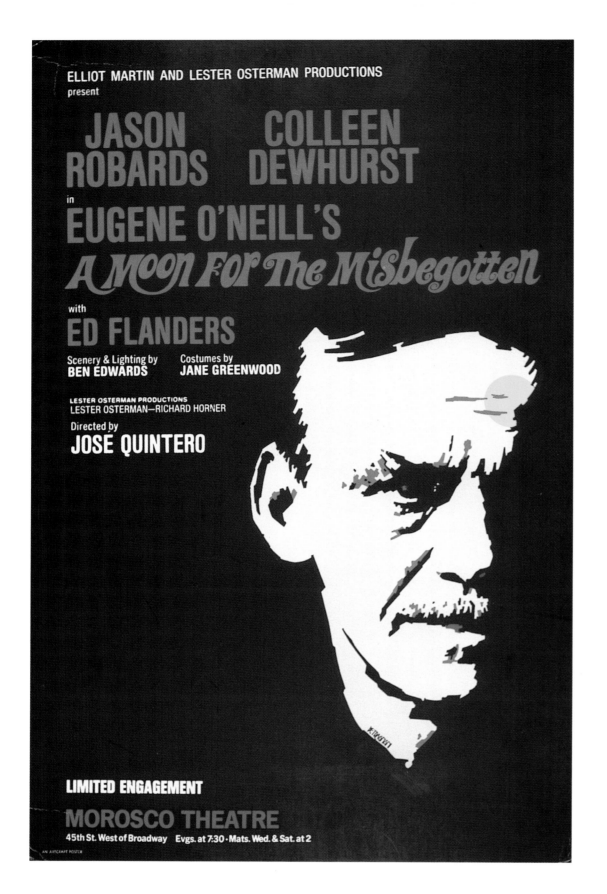

A Moon for the Misbegotten, 1973
Window card
*Courtesy Performing Arts Research Center
The New York Public Library at Lincoln Center*

Equus, 1974
Windowcard designed by Gilbert Lesser
*Museum of the City of New York, The Theater
Collection*

EQUUS
Plymouth Theatre

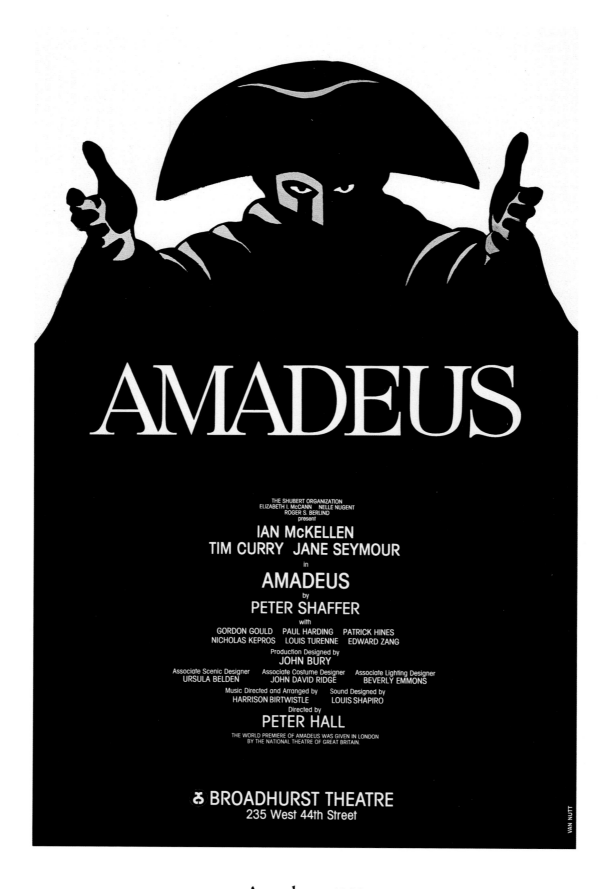

VAN NUTT

Amadeus, 1980
Window card
Private Collection

Rocky Horror Show, 1980
Window card
Private Collection

Give our regards to Broadway— and tell them we're on our way! *Rocky*

Lou Adler Presents
The Michael White Production
Starring
Tim Curry
in
THE ROCKY HORROR SHOW

THE BEAUTIFUL BELASCO
44th St. East of B'way

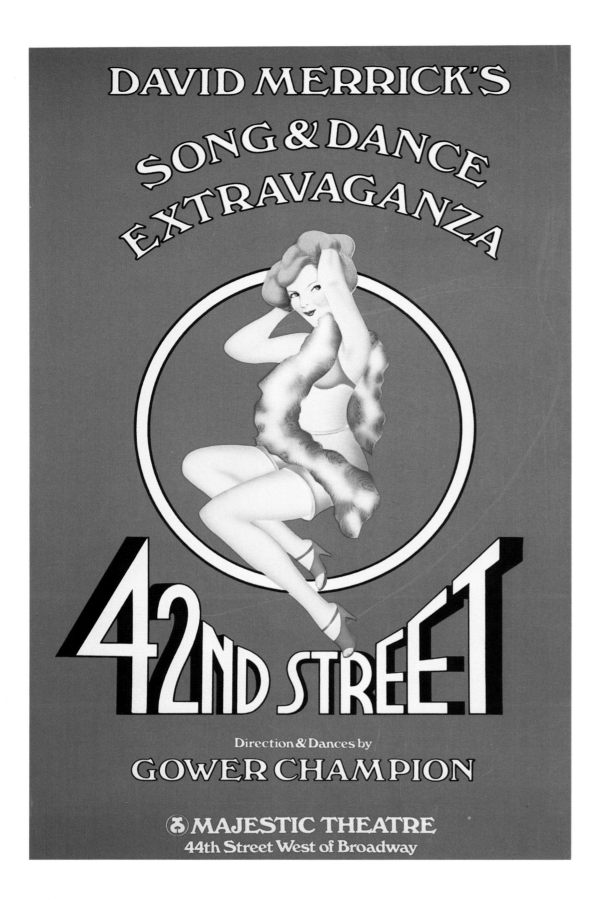

42nd Street, 1981
Window card
Courtesy Performing Arts Research Center
The New York Public Library at Lincoln Center

Cats, 1982
Poster designed and printed by Dewynters plc
© TM 1981 The Really Useful Group Ltd
Photolithograph
22 × 13⅞ inches (55.9 × 35.3 cm)
Private Collection

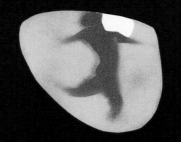

CATS

MUSIC BY ANDREW LLOYD WEBBER
BASED ON 'OLD POSSUM'S BOOK OF PRACTICAL CATS' BY T. S. ELIOT

PRESENTED BY   CAMERON MACKINTOSH,   THE REALLY USEFUL COMPANY
LIMITED,   DAVID GEFFEN   AND   THE SHUBERT ORGANIZATION

THE "CATS" COMPANY: (IN ALPHABETICAL ORDER)
KENNETH ARD,   BETTY BUCKLEY,   RENÉ CEBALLOS,   WALTER CHARLES,
RENÉ CLEMENTE,   MARLÈNE DANIELLE,   WENDY EDMEAD,   DIANE
FRATANTONI,   STEVEN GELFER,   HARRY GROENER,   STEVEN HACK,
STEPHEN HANAN,   ROBERT HOSHOUR,   JANET L. HUBERT,   REED JONES,
WHITNEY KERSHAW,   DONNA KING,   CHRISTINE LANGNER,   TERRENCE V.
MANN,   ANNA McNEELY,   HECTOR JAIME MERCADO,   BOB MORRISEY,
CYNTHIA ONRUBIA,   KEN PAGE,   SUSAN POWERS,   CAROL RICHARDS,   JOEL
ROBERTSON,   TIMOTHY SCOTT,   HERMAN W. SEBEK,   BONNIE SIMMONS

EXECUTIVE PRODUCERS   R. TYLER GATCHELL, JR.,   PETER NEUFELD,
ORCHESTRATIONS BY DAVID CULLEN   AND   ANDREW LLOYD WEBBER,
PRODUCTION MUSICAL DIRECTOR   STANLEY LEBOWSKY,   MUSICAL
DIRECTOR RENE WIEGERT,   SOUND DESIGN BY **MARTIN LEVAN,**   LIGHTING
DESIGN BY **DAVID HERSEY,**   DESIGNED BY **JOHN NAPIER,**   ASSOCIATE
DIRECTOR AND CHOREOGRAPHER **GILLIAN LYNNE,**   DIRECTED BY **TREVOR NUNN.**

ORIGINAL CAST ALBUM ON GEFFEN RECORDS & TAPES ☺
♿ **WINTER GARDEN THEATRE**
50TH STREET & BROADWAY · NEW YORK

SUNDAY in the PARK with GEORGE

A Musical

The Shubert Organization and Emanuel Azenberg
by arrangement with
Playwrights Horizons
present

Mandy   Bernadette
Patinkin Peters
in

SUNDAY in the PARK with GEORGE
A Musical

Music and Lyrics by
Stephen Sondheim

Book by
James Lapine

Scenery by	Costumes by	Lighting by
Tony	Patricia Ann	Richard
Straiges	Zipprodt and Hould-Ward	Nelson

Special Effects by	Sound by	Hair and Makeup
Bran Ferren	Tom Morse	Lo Presto/Allen

Musical Direction by	Orchestrations by	Movement by
Paul	Michael	Randolyn
Gemignani	Starobin	Zinn

Directed by
James Lapine

Ⓢ Booth Theatre 45th Street West of Broadway

© FRAVER 1984

Into the Woods, 1987
Window card
*Courtesy Performing Arts Research Center
The New York Public Library at Lincoln Center*

Sunday in the Park with George, 1984
Window card
*Museum of the City of New York, The Theater
Collection*

Miss Saigon, 1991
Poster designed and printed by Dewynters plc TM for
Cameron Mackintosh Limited TM © 1988 CML
Photolithograph
22 × 13⅞ inches (55.9 × 35.3 cm)
Private Collection

Jelly's Last Jam, 1992
Window card
*Museum of the City of New York, The Theater
Collection*

GREGORY HINES
Margo Lion and Pamela Koslow
in association with
PolyGram Diversified Entertainment,
126 Second Ave Corp./Hal Luftig, Rodger Hess,
Jujamcyn Theaters/TV Asahi
and Herb Alpert
present
GREGORY HINES
in
JELLY'S LAST JAM
Book by George C. Wolfe
Music by Jelly Roll Morton
Lyrics by Susan Birkenhead
Musical Adaptation and Additional Music Composed by
Luther Henderson
with
(in alphabetical order)
Savion Glover Stanley Wayne Mathis Tonya Pinkins
and
Mary Bond Davis Mamie Duncan-Gibbs Ann Duquesnay
Stephanie Pope Ruben Santiago-Hudson Allison Williams
Ken Ard Adrian Bailey Clare Bathé Sherry D. Boone Bill Brassea Brenda Braxton
Ralph Deaton Melissa Haizlip Lawrence Hamilton Cee-Cee Harshaw
Janice Lorraine Holt Don Johanson Ted L. Levy Victoria Gabrielle Platt
Gil Pritchett III Ken Roberson Michelle M. Robinson La-Rose Saxon
Jimmy W. Tate Gordon Joseph Weiss
and
Keith David
Scenic Design Robin Wagner
Costume Design Toni-Leslie James
Lighting Design Jules Fisher
Musical Supervision and Orchestrations Luther Henderson
Musical Direction Linda Twine
Musical Coordinator John Miller
Sound Design Otts Munderloh
Mask & Puppet Design Barbara Pollitt
Hair Design Jeffrey Frank
Executive Producer David Strong Warner, Inc.
Production Stage Manager Arturo E. Porazzi
Casting Hughes/Moss
Technical Supervisor Francis A. Hauser
Press Representation Richard Kornberg
Associate Producers
Peggy Hill Rosenkranz Marilyn Hall Dentsu Inc., New York
Tap Choreography
Gregory Hines and Ted L. Levy
Choreography
Hope Clarke
Directed by
George C. Wolfe
Originally Produced by Center Theatre Group of Los Angeles
at the Mark Taper Forum, Gordon Davidson, Artistic Director
Charles Dillingham, Managing Director.
Wolf
© 1992 Serino Coyne Inc. Art: Wolfgang Kuhl
JELLY'S LAST JAM
Virginia Theatre, 245 West 52nd Street

ACKNOWLEDGMENTS

The publisher would like to thank Martin Bristow, who designed this book, Elizabeth Montgomery, who did the picture research, and Jessica Hodge, the editor. We would also like to thank the following institutions and agencies for supplying photographic material.

American Antiquarian Society, Worcester, Mass: page 6
Antique Poster Collection Gallery, Ridgefield, C.T.: pages 29, 30, 32, 34, 35, 38, 39, 40, 41, 42, 43, 44, 45, 46/47, 49, 53, 54/55
Beinecke Rare Book and Manuscript Library, Yale University: pages 55, 56, 57, 58, 59, 64, 65, 67, 77, 85
Bettmann Archive: pages 8 (left below, right above, right below), 9 (right), 10 (bottom), 11 (left), 12 (bottom), 15 (above), 21 (left)
Brompton Picture Library: pages 12 (left), 24, 25
George Mason University, Fairfax, VA: pages 23 (both), 71, 72, 74, 75
Harry Ransom Humanities Research Center, the University of Texas at Austin, Theatre Arts Collection: pages 2, 9 (left), 13, 21 (right), 22, 26, 31, 33, 51, 88, 92, 99
Harvard Theatre Collection: pages 7, 8 (left above), 20
The Metropolitan Museum of Art: pages 36/37 (Gift of Fern Bradley Dufner, 1952, 52.625.143), 52 (Gift of A J Kobler, 1920)
Museum of the City of New York, Theater Collection: pages 11 (right above and right below), 12 (right), 18, 48, 50, 60, 62, 68, 69, 70, 73, 79, 81, 82, 83, 87, 94, 95, 96, 103, 104, 106, 108, 109, 111
New-York Historical Society NYC: page 52
New York Public Library at Lincoln Center, Performing Arts Research Center: pages 27, 28, 61, 63, 66, 76, 81, 84, 89, 90, 91, 98, 100, 102
Private collection: pages 97, 101, 105, 111
Royal Shakespeare Company Collection: page 10 (above)
Springer/Bettmann Film Archive: pages 14 (below), 15 (below), 17 (above), 19 (both)
UPI/Bettmann: pages 14 (above), 16, 17 (below)